# Capture My Heart, Educate My Soul

**A Training and Reflection Manual for Faculty of Developmental English Students and Faculty Teaching Gatekeeper Courses**

# CAPTURE MY HEART, EDUCATE MY SOUL

A Training and Reflection Manual for Faculty of Developmental English Students and Faculty Teaching Gatekeeper Courses

## Pamela Tolbert-Bynum Rivers, Ed.D

Hopewell Publications

Published by Hopewell
Publications, LLC
PO Box 11, Titusville, NJ
08560-0011
(609) 818-1049

info@HopePubs.com
www.HopePubs.com

International Standard Book Number: 9781933435527

Library of Congress Control Number: 2018950623

First Edition

Printed in the United States of America

Dedicated to the people of Gary, Indiana,
and the late Dharathula "Dolly" H. Millender—
librarian, author, historian, and keeper of the faith.

## DISCLAIMER

The biographical vignettes in this work are composites and
not actual people. They are utilized to better understand
certain phenomena, such as accountability and motivation.
Individual privacy and anonymity have been preserved.
Throughout this book, the terms "developmental education"
and "remedial education" are used interchangeably.

**C** are about me

**A** ttend to me

**P** ersuade me

**T** ransform me

**U** nderstand me

**R** espect me

**E** ngage me

**...My Heart, Educate My Soul**

# Table of Contents

# Foreword

*Capture My Heart, Educate My Soul* is a compelling call to action for faculty and administrators to explore high impact practices and strategies that promote educational equity through caring and culturally-responsive teaching (CRT). The manual... presents a much appreciated and much-needed strengths-based approach to teaching and learning.

The transparent manner in which the author narrates and reflects upon her own educational journey is inspiring and beautiful. The concept of authentic and transformational academics is particularly fascinating, and the CAPTURE acronym is quite meaningful.

Additionally, the adult learning theories presented are important and add value to the text. As content experts, so many community college faculty are not exposed to and taught adult learning theories, and this guide reinforces those professional development needs. The strategies provided will help all developmental education faculty, revealing what many likely wish they would have known prior to teaching, i.e. setting the tone and example in the first few weeks. CAPTURE presents the possibilities of what educators can do, when so many deem reaching struggling students a hopeless endeavor. Contrarily, the author encourages developmental education faculty members and praises their work, despite the stigma often associated with teaching developmental education courses. Likewise, meaningful is the emphasis that she places on the importance of faculty reflection and self-awareness. Her notion of the authentic educator, under girded by morals and spirituality, resonates!

**Monica Walker, Ed.D.**
Dean, Developmental Education &
Special Academic Programs
The Community College of Baltimore

# Preface

Capture my heart, and then educate my soul. In so doing, you unlock the potential in me to turn the world upside down. Me—the adult developmental education student who came to you barely able to compose a complete sentence in English. You know me. I'm undocumented, so I may not look you in the eye. I may be sleeping in my car, but you can't see "homelessness" in me, unless you know where to look. I may be ashamed because I don't always comprehend what I read; or I may very well be angry at the universe because now I know "they" just let me slide through high school to play football or encouraged my dropping out to boost standardized test averages, and I'm regretful of so many things I did because I didn't know. I didn't know because nobody ever told me, so now I'm trying to play catch up, at a time when nobody's really giving me a chance to catch up. I'm running out of energy, patience, and out of money. This is it for me. This is *el final de la línea* (i.e. the end of the line).

# Introduction

This book is not a research study, although three specific adult learning theories provide a conceptual framework for approaching or understanding many of the strategies, applications, and attitudes contained herein. Such theories include andragogy, transformative learning, and experiential learning theory. These theories focus on meeting adult students where they are in life, as multi-faceted learners who are rich in prior experiences, and intimately connected to their cultural landscape, communities, families, and other significant social entities. Often, these entities provide a critical lens through which most adults perceive and make meaning of life. Clearly, we must understand the significance of these entities, for they are not peripheral to the learning that takes place in adult settings. Rather, they are central to it. They provide shape to many of the non-cognitive attitudes and skill sets adult learners possess. As adult educators, we need the ability and willingness to tap into these underappreciated attitudes and skill sets, that we might build upon them. If we do not understand this, we will miss the mark, and do a disservice to our students.

As such, the aim of this particular manual is not to critique or even broaden the current field of research around developmental education and its higher education students. There is more than enough research to identify and validate the struggles and concerns of underprepared students in higher education, or those who place into developmental education courses. This information is well documented. (Please see the References list in *Part V - Appendix*.) Rather, this is a toolbox of practical measures, strategies, and reflections undergirded by practice, research, and theory. It serves as a culturally-relevant alternative to traditional developmental education strategies and supplemental forms of instruction, with an unapologetic focus on African-American students, who disproportionately make up the majority of students placed into two-year or four-year college developmental courses.

Although this work is not a research study, as noted, the data is compelling and heartbreaking enough to warrant attention. Developmental educational is intended as a sequence of courses and strategies that will assist those students who are underprepared for the academic rigor of college-level coursework. Such students are perceived to be starting out at an academic or cognitive deficit, and many are. We have known of remedial education's consequences for nearly fifty years. However, considering the unprecedented world-wide competition for jobs, rapid-paced technological advances, and global unrest of every type, there is a crisis at hand, prompting an immediate call to action. We stand to lose an entire generation to continued economic inequality and workforce malaise should we choose to turn a blind eye to the reality and consequences of students of color who enroll in remedial courses, or fail the gatekeeper courses. The data reports on individuals, but failure destabilizes and impacts the well-being of entire families, communities, and cities, on a number of levels.

According to a 2016 study by Chen and Simone, at public two-year colleges, "78 percent of Black students, 75 percent of Hispanic students, and 64 percent of White students take remedial courses... At public four-year colleges, 66 percent of

Black students, 53 percent of Hispanic students, and 36 percent of White students take remedial courses.[1] Further sobering, a 2016 report from Complete College America "indicates that 20% of students placed in remedial education at two-year colleges, and 36% of their counterparts at four-year colleges complete a remedial education course within two years. Additionally, only 22% of students who complete remedial education courses complete the associated gateway subject course: for example, a first-level English or math course.."[2] Moreover, "this reality is disproportionately true for low-income students and students of color..."[3] The college success disparities are disturbing, particularly, although not exclusively, at community colleges, prompting some re-searchers to deem remedial education as the "systemic black hole from which students are unlikely to emerge.."[4] For many students of color, it is the first course they take upon college matriculation, and it may very well be their last, for many pay for these non-credit courses with loans, and leave college without a degree, and in debt.

Thus, the overarching goal of this work is to assist in leveling the playing field for such students by encouraging, equipping, and training those faculty members and administrators who are charged to competently educate them in collegiate settings, while maintaining the same high intellectual standards and expectations afforded all other students.

It is worth noting that these attitudes and techniques are not much different from those used to facilitate the learning of honors students or the exceptionally motivated. They can, in fact, be modified to teach any specialized group of adult learners when the emphasis is not merely on the perceived weaknesses or need, but rather, on the unique strengths and gifts of the group. If one's focus is solely, or even primarily, on the needs—or conversely, on the "assumed" kinesthetic gifts—we will neglect the opportunity to nurture teachable moments, and we will lose many of these students before they can even begin.

With this in mind, faculty of adult learners who place into developmental education must be particularly attentive of the need to bring the whole self into the classroom, and not merely the academic self, which is just a marginal facet of who we are as professors anyway. Much of the purely academic content presented to students is accessible on the internet. To complement and add value, we must bring the whole self to the teaching/learning transaction.

This is to say, bring the self that cares for these students in and outside of the classroom. Bring the self that understands these students. You have stood in their shoes as a working adult, caring for children—and perhaps parents simultaneous-ly—or as the spouse to such a student, or as one challenged by life in any number of ways. If you are or were a blue-collar worker and have no thoughts of subjugating those hard-earned values and lived experiences for the tenets of hegemony, bring that to your instruction. Bring your proud, working-class ethic to the classroom and to the administrative table. Bring everything you know about life, survival, persistence, self-love, and self-respect. Everything that supports your students in their journey and endeavors, bring that to the table, and present it to them as if these students were your very own family. That's how we support them holistically, because if not us, who will?

Many of our adult students who place into developmental education courses and certain "gatekeeper" courses lack foundational, basic supports. Some researchers—who may have, surprisingly, never taught a remedial course, and do not remotely mirror this population—take this for granted when analyzing aggregate data and surmising their findings and recommendations. They may not consider the very real fact that mature, nontraditional students often come to us educationally deficient and may have significant gaps in their learning because they are still contending with the repercussions of deeply rooted wounds, traumas, or instabilities that were far beyond their control. Some may suffer PTSD in ways we cannot imagine. They may lack intellectual confidence, not because they lack intellectual capital —after all, they survive on a daily basis—but because they were coerced into feeling intellectually defective based on disadvantages, errant thinking processes, or systemic factors outside of their control.

Let us reasonably consider that 12-year old Mary carried the emotional brunt of her entire family when her mother sank into a depression years ago and could not adequately care for her children. Mary's choices were to complete homework without internet access or care for two younger siblings. She lacked the will and support to do it all. Perhaps Mary left high school sometime afterwards, dropping out when she legally could do so, to work and raise a family, and then years later acquiring her GED before enrolling in community college, where she placed into developmental English and math. Now as an adult learner, although her cognitive abilities may be limited, her metacognitive skills are intensified as she learned to function in society and manage a household. These life management skills, not her deficiencies, should be acknowledged, targeted, and then deliberately and creatively employed, to bring Mary to a point where she is confident enough in her abilities to engage with new academic learning and skills.  do this by raising the bar of Mary's academic dexterity, not lowering it, because as an adult with life experience under her belt, Mary will surely recognize or sense the lowering of standards and the adjustment in expectations, but she will also recognize her ability to succeed or at least survive. We do this by demonstrating to Mary the intellectual—and thus academic and practical—value of her daily skills and habits, how to deconstruct those daily skills into consumable chunks, and then ignite those parts to fuel a comprehension of foreign concepts. In essence, we teach Mary metacognition processes. We teach Mary, and others like her, the value in dissecting, analyzing, and ultimately controlling how she thinks about learning. When many of our developmental education students come to embrace their devalued survival tactics as genius measures on their own, power is unleashed.

Yet, how do we get there with learners like Mary? Research supports the notion that for most students, instructor authenticity is key to developing the rapport necessary for this type of individual and classroom success. Yet, it rarely develops in one semester. The old adage "people don't care what you know until they know that you care" is true for the vast majority of individuals. It is true for developmental students. It is true for lifelong learners. It is true for millennials. Authenticity is a core requisite, as is ethical care, and other professional and personal attributes discussed later in this manual. My students often tell me that they like my style. What they mean is that they like (and appreciate) my confidence in them and valuation of their life experiences.

However, regardless of one's professional ethics, let us be clear. As faculty, you will not reach every student. Every student will not respond to you or your methods. Yet, try anyway. Never give up on anyone.

Many students entering developmental education courses have little to no true academic success, for any number of reasons. Thus, as educators, we do not give up in refining our methods. Again, to level this playing field, bring your *whole* self into the classroom, not just your academic self. What mature developmental education students need from you is three-fold:

1. critical thinking proficiency (the ability to analyze and synthesize in a complex world),

2. positionality perspective, (an epistemological foundation for the establishment of agency in adult learners), and

3. metacognition validation (an acknowledgement and valuation of subliminal "coping" strategies and techniques that enable one to scaffold prior learning and more readily acquire new learning).

## Too Much at Stake

I know from personal experience. I am an African American educator who was lifted out of many debilitating forms of poverty and despair by my community of origin. It was the community that loved and lifted me not merely out of financial poverty, which ebbs and flows, but out of a multiplicity of root poverties that, had I not overcome them, may have flourished in various iterations for much of my adult life, enabling all manner of self-defeating behaviors and potentially devastating pathologies. The community did this through the vehicle of education. I was one of five siblings raised on public assistance by a single parent. Today, I possess four degrees, two from Ivy League universities, including an earned doctorate from one of the nation's premier schools of education. Once I acquired these credentials, the decision to educate those from similar humble origins came instinctively, and I discovered the mission of community colleges later in life. These open access institutions, and others like them I discovered, had been accepting and transforming the lives of adult learners on the margins of life for decades, regardless of their GPA or standardized test score. Today, I educate at these institutions because I want to be there. I had support, counseling, and choices around higher education when I graduated from high school, although many of my students do not and did not. I choose to teach at least one developmental English course each semester because I know these students, and teaching them is my reasonable service. To serve them is to serve those who lifted me, and it is not a responsibility to be taken lightly.

In many institutions of higher education, the teaching of developmental education students has traditionally been assigned to adjunct or part-time faculty, arguably the most dedicated, unsung members of the professoriate. Indeed, most institutions of higher education could not function nor survive without the service and scholarship of these esteemed individuals. However, this steadfast group also has traditionally had very little control over institutional or departmental scheduling and budgetary allocations. As a result, for lack of professional development opportunities alone, they may be the least prepared to teach such students. This paradigm needs to be shifted immediately. If we schedule such courses to those who are willing, prepared, or even inspired to teach developmental students, they will find creative, efficacious, and intelligent ways to teach them. They will capture the hearts of their students in order to educate their souls as something innately pedagogical.

Recently, when one junior faculty member learned that she had been scheduled to teach a Freshman Composition course in lieu of developmental English, her delighted, albeit misguided, response was, "I guess I've been promoted!" This is an unfortunate, yet not uncommon mentality for so many faculty members who, immersed in academic protocol and mores, feel that the teaching of students who are under-prepared for the rigors of college is somehow "less than." Subconsciously, the assignment to teach developmental courses and students is then perceived of as a devaluation of their pedigrees and intellectual capacity. For the insecure or inexperienced faculty member, the translation becomes "If I teach students who are 'less than,' I must be considered 'less than' in the eyes of the college, which is not a place where I want to be." To counter this mentality, we must prepare and value faculty for this population, just as we prepare and openly esteem faculty assigned to the teaching of our honors students, ESL students, and any other specialized cohort or learning community, even when methodology design is similarly rigorous. When value is constructively assessed, faculty respond in like manner.

Yet, historically, despite our best efforts, we simply cannot deny the reality of underprepared students still coming to the nation's colleges and universities in droves, as high school graduates or with equivalency diplomas in hand. Regardless, although we prepare to instruct such students, this is not by any means to suggest that such a reality is ever acceptable. Nor should any facilitating steps mentioned in this work be construed as normalization measures. To be clear, although mature students may require a refresher course after an academic hiatus, there is nothing normal about newly-minted high school "graduates" paying to acquire secondary-level skills with their post-secondary tuition dollars. The teaching of developmental courses in the collegiate setting, and the intake of tuition dollars to support this instruction, should not only be understood as an anomaly, but an injustice to the student, for it flies deeply in the face of his/her right to an equal educational opportunity. In this case, if education is a *process* that should end in the acquisition of knowledge, common and foundational for a certain level, we have indefensibly failed these students. And if people are a society's most valuable resource, don't we want the best outcome for all?

# Part I – Laying the Foundation

## CARE About Me

There was a young woman who grew up in the Bronx, in a home where unpaid bills and disconnect notices rained on the dining room table each month, and on everybody's parade. Her father slapped her mother. Her mother slapped her. She berated her boyfriend, who comforted her before the baby came. And then married her, and slapped her, and hospitalized her twice. He threatened her on the ledge of a fire escape and shoved her against a brick wall, making up with her many times before the next two babies came. When her nose was finally broken and she awakened, bruised and in pain, at the hospital emergency ward, her soul also awakened.

Something beautiful and fierce aroused that day, cracked open its shell, opened its eyes, and declared, like baby's breath: I am here. I am still here.

*My name is Hope on good days.*
*My name is Faith on freedom days.*
*My name is Resilience on impossible days.*
*And my name is Honor today, and always.*
*And I am here. I am still here.*

Honor was almost 30-years-old when she made her way into my developmental English classroom one bright

September morning. Honor had managed to file separation papers against her husband only six months ago, and now she lived three buildings away from her mother, on the corner of 157th Street and Grand Concourse. She had dropped off her two youngest children in daycare, and one into kindergarten, before arriving five minutes early to class, sliding into a seat on the front row where the vagrant twins anxiety and depression waited for her, laughing at her and tugging at her sleeve. But she had already made up her mind to shrug them off and smile, because Resilience knew her name this morning, and had also chosen to accompany her on this day, the first day of her brand-new life.

## Adult Learning Theories Overview

**Andragogy:** The term andragogy was first used in 1833 by German educator Alexander Kapp. However, the theory was developed by adult educator Malcolm Knowles as the art and science of any adult learning. Knowles' adult learning theory of andragogy (i.e. man-leading, as opposed to pedagogy, which means child-leading) is predicated upon the following four principles that are applicable to this manual, and distinguish adult learning from other forms of learning:

1. Adults should be involved in their own instruction and education.

2. Experiences provide the foundation for true adult learning.

3. Adults are most engaged by learning that is immediately applicable to their lives.

4. Adult learning is most focused on problem-solving, as opposed to merely acquiring content knowledge.

## Transformative Learning

Transformative or transformational learning is the process of learning how to transform or change problematic frames of reference to make them more inclusive, broader, or whole. It is about how adults interpret or make meaning of their world and circumstances. In essence, it is "an epistemology of how adults learn to think for themselves, rather than act upon the assimilated beliefs, values, feelings, and judgments of others.[5] These transformative experiences adults have in life have the capacity to cause a shift in consciousness, behaviors, and even lifestyle. Epiphanius moments leave a lasting impression, allowing adults to reimagine old experiences in a new light, and critically reflect to make intelligent meaning of current beliefs and attitudes. It is a three-step process entailing the identification of *crisis triggers* or areas where we have held on to erroneous belief systems or mindsets; followed by learning that has personal or professional relevance to the adult; and finally followed by learning based on critical reflection, which allows adults the opportunity to reconsider, tweak, or even discard long-established beliefs and values.[6]

## Experiential Learning

Experiential learning is, as its name suggests, learning that is grounded in experience. Although individuals may learn from textbooks and from other individuals, experiential learning theory insists that the "essence of adult learning is making sense of experiences",[7] particularly powerful experiences that are not easily forgotten. For example, according to experiential learning theory, adults need kinesthetic learning exercises, such as simulations and realistic scenarios; demonstrations, examinations and reflections on case studies; role-playing and other "learning by doing" activities; as well as any activity that allows them to make meaning of a concept based on personal relevance. It is most important for adults to self-internalize learning based on how the learning is relevant to their life and circumstances. However, although many contemporary adult education theorists have a concise understanding of this connection between experience and learning, they also understand that "this form of knowledge is highly influenced by socio-cultural and historical factors."[8]

# Conceptions of Authenticity, Care, and Humor in the Context of Adult Learning

Authenticity in the classroom is an often-misunderstood ideal that is reviewed in the literature from various perspectives and often found to be synonymous with an ethic of care. However, practical guidelines for promoting this nebulous concept are few, partially due to the difficulty of understanding what it means to be authentic in the classroom, or in any adult learning environment. Some will rightly argue that in our litigious and complex world, the discerning educator will refrain from divulging too much of one's personal life.

This concept of authenticity, and the various means by which it is generated and actualized in the classroom, is much theorized in the literature as an academic construct with highly political overtones. Authenticity has been linked philosophically with Paulo Freire's sense of "conscientization" (1971) and Carl Jung's "individuation" (1973). Among some educators, it is often regarded as the multi-layered central tenet in the process of transformational learning, at once a goal associated with self-awareness or self-empowerment, a process of human development undergirded by a moral or spiritual framework, and simultaneously a teaching modality. For the sake of usage in this work, it is regarded as the latter: a simple modality to be adopted by those with experience and wisdom.

Postmodernist/poststructuralist educators and thinkers might rightly take issue with the validity of the concept altogether, noting humanity's various socialization processes and the fluidity of the *self* as a result. Such individuals might always challenge the notion of a unified authentic self in the face of race, class, and gender orientations. Yet always the unanswered question is, even if one could uniquely and consensually define the concept, what does authentic, transformational teaching and learning look like, and result in? In essence, to what extent might engaged instructional methods, particularly humor, and the presence of a competent and an authentic facilitator play in the success of the modern adult learner, regardless of the venue?

The intent is to understand authenticity in the context of adult and higher education with a focus on one obvious dimension of authenticity, and that being the role of the affective in teaching and learning. Much of the literature on adult learning theory, and transformational learning in particular, has come under fire for emphasizing and elevating cognitive processes over the affective realm, and much of this criticism has come from the perspective of postmodernist thinkers who have made note of how structural and contextual factors and inequalities alter how we teach, why we teach, to whom we teach, and even how authentic we are allowed to be in our teaching relationships. Indeed, to honestly reflect upon and make meaning of authenticity and how this might translate to authentic *care* in the classroom, we now know that the focus on cognition alone is ineffective.

"'Does this ring true,' 'does this feel right,' and 'is this what education in the end is all about,' are important questions to attend to."[9] The answers to many of these questions hinge upon the affective domain in teaching and learning and arise out of what Nel Noddings (1984) has termed *ethical caring*[10], which is essentially a state of being in relation with others, characterized by receptivity, relatedness and engrossment.[11]

This elevation of the affective realm is also a product of the recognition that care and authenticity are often written about and understood from a Eurocentric point of view, which has traditionally elevated cognition over non-cognitive attributes. With the exception of prominent educators such as bell hooks, who is African American, little had been written or published from "other" canons, traditions, and cultures that might typically consider authenticity as an "emotionally-charged"[12] affair. What it *feels like* to be authentic would take precedence over reflection, discourse, and traditional means of awareness. "I believe this," "these are my values because I was raised this way," or "it is ingrained in my spirit" are responses not necessarily birthed out of critical reflection.

As such, Parker Palmer (1998) linked authenticity with integrity and a sense of selfhood. The authentic educator knows who he or she is and is comfortable and secure in his or her own skin. As a result, he or she is able to penetrate and engage a broader array of students, doing what feels like it is in the best interest of learners. Patricia Cranton (2001) agreed with this assessment and suggested that to find one's identity *is* to become more authentic.

Conversely, the inauthentic educator relies upon theory and prescribed pedagogical methods and avoids risks, perhaps fearing retaliation by colleagues for not being scholarly enough, often undermining her own potential efficacy and power in the adult learning setting, not to mention the epiphanies her students might have enjoyed. One might assume that the inauthentic educator does not particularly care for his or her students; however, one could also argue that the care is superficial at best or simply not based in a moral chasm for which we assume it would be. According to Martin Heidegger, "one can authentically exist without being moral, and act morally without authentically existing."[13] This thought carries over for the adult educator, as well.

Patricia Cranton sees authenticity as the "expression of one's genuine self" and "an authentic teacher as someone who merges self and teacher, bringing him or herself into the teaching or into the relationships with students."[14] Similarly, Palmer described authentic teachers or those who have integrity, as having "a capacity to bring about vital connec-tions between teacher and subject,... teacher and student,...

and student and subject..."[15] This sense of authenticity is morally or spiritually based and serves as the foundation for the care displayed by some educators.

Writing in 1991, Charles Taylor indicated that authenticity for the educator entailed an "openness to horizons of significance"[16] and that this horizon of significance provided the boundary around which one would attempt to define the self in the quest for an authentic identity. Choices related to pedagogy and classroom ethics are then informed by one's personal horizons of significance and, more importantly, one's educational philosophy is ultimately defined based on those horizons. For example, educators who declare their service of teaching for social change have already described their horizon.

Philosopher Nel Noddings observed that true, authentically based caring, "in the most significant sense, is to help [another] grow and actualize himself."[17] Yet, this is certainly risk-based caring. While superficial caring adheres to rules and regulations, regardless of how they may affect the individual, authentic caring requires that the educator transcend known boundaries or even "break established rules." Jarvis (1992) is also clear in his acknowledgement of the link between care and the desire for positive development of the other. He observed that "authentic action is to be found when individuals freely act in such a way that they try to foster the growth and development of each other's being."[18] Jarvis then went on to note that authentic teachers would promote the development of authenticity in others. It is reasonable to assume that the authentic teacher would want to encourage that authenticity by any logical means, including the utilization of humor.

Cranton & Caruseta (2004) used a grounded theory approach to their research with 22 educators over three years and determined that the five dimensions of authenticity for educators are "self-awareness, awareness of others, relationships with learners, awareness of context, and a critically reflective approach to practice."[19] Implicit in this list is a moral sense of caring; an ethos of care that regards students as one would regard self. This morality-based caring often emanates from social action theorists who view education as intrinsically a liberating force.

## Social Action and Authenticity

The social action theory of adult learning, or radical adult education, is essentially predicated upon the notion that education in the truest sense must be about the raising of an individual's consciousness to the inequities or imbalances in life. It is what Freire (1970) termed "conscientization."[20] It was based on a situation of political, social, and economic oppression in Freire's native Brazil. However, from that time to contemporary times, educators throughout the world, who believe such a system exists on some level in most governmental structures, have embraced and utilized the theory.

Moreover, many minority students, due to their positionality in relation to dominant cultures, are more likely to have experienced and can confirm Freire's description of oppression. That education and success for these individuals entails a consciousness-raising that is apart from economic success should not be surprising. It must also be acknowledged that these individuals strive against, in large measure, and on a daily basis, what Patricia Collins (2000) described as "controlling images"[21] that strongly influence one's perception of success. For such students, personal success may be only marginally related to economic power.

According to black feminist literature, the objectification of black Americans can be traced back to slavery in the Americas and is indicative of a need to have some group serve as the marginalized, the insignificant, or the binary *other*." Essentially, the existence of the *other* concretizes and establishes the norm to which all should aspire. The notion that certain of our students struggle within this framework sheds light upon the reality of experience. Furthermore, all of the competencies society perceives of as necessary for success require that certain students struggle against common stereotypes.

For example, Collins' depictions of the past and present controlling images presented to objectify black women—such as nursing mammies, emasculating matriarchs, or welfare queens—are quite clear and significant. This objectification of stereotypes is pernicious, as *dualistic thinking* contends that the objectified is always the negative binary. When the media reinforces these images in the minds of individuals—most potently when they are visually and indelibly etched via television, social media, etc.—the stereotype becomes the norm or the undisputed, and those relegated to "other" often assume a defensive stance that is psychologically and emotionally draining.

Moreover, delving into the literature on adult development, one can conclude that certain students find themselves in the position of *receiver* of knowledge, as defined by Belenky et al. (1986)[22]. For some individuals, knowledge is rarely subjectively derived. These individuals look towards some external authority, and that authority provides the knowledge, which they then receive as ultimate truth. These individuals are not capable of questioning what they receive via the authoritative media. Like the "naïve dualist" described by educator Knefelkamp (1996), the notion of externality is quite crucial for the receiver. Knefelkamp specifies characteristics of dualism and notes that for the dualist thinker, "knowledge is related to absolute truth handed down from external forces often quite removed from those receiving the knowledge."[23] Knowledge is a black/white, either/or proposition because there is the longing for truth and one seeks that truth outside of self, from authoritarian figures. Knefelkamp describes this seeking as a process that is natural in human development. It is not pernicious (as opposed to naïve dualism), for it is not a deliberate way of thinking and being; it is a transitional way of assessing one's world.

The adult development literature is also informed by Perry (1999) who argued that dualism and contingent thinking should be viewed as "characteristics of stages in the development process itself."[24] For the traditional college students interviewed by Perry, dualistic thinking was primarily naïve dualism; they would learn and grow to question and contest how images are presented to them, what they represent, who controls the images and, most importantly, who benefits from them. However, when controlling images are presented over and over again to those who have adopted dualistic thinking as a conscious, permanent place to be in the fashioning of their life perspectives, it becomes dangerous and problematic for society. The ramifications are profoundly pernicious in their effect upon the groups/ individuals stereotyped, as well as those who choose to think this way. This is true for the nontraditional adult student, or the underprepared adult student, who can be understood in light of what Perry examines, for these students may often find themselves in positions where they are responding to the dualistic thinking of others.

Social theorist Richards is quoted as noting intense objectification to be a "prerequisite for the despiritualization of the universe" (in Collins).[25] However, despite what adult students confront on a daily basis, despite the onslaught of negative, media-controlled images and other negative external variables, a competent, caring instructor; development of non-cognitive skills; and overall maturity in the student are factors not to be disregarded. The literature again points to Kegan (2002) and others who acknowledge that an individual's ability to be "self-authored"[26] allows him or her to more readily make choices that are parallel with his or her own personal value system, in lieu of values that are socially constructed and often introduced subliminally. One may hypothesize that age has much to do with one's ability to follow his or her own personal sense of that which is right, acceptable, or just. Perry's stages of intellectual development may well have implications for the adult student, in that age and maturity must be taken into account when one considers the position and measure of intelligence.

In addition, positionality and power are critical adult development concepts that come into play in the lives of students who are primarily ethnic minorities and women. French & Raven (1960) espoused five types of power and considered the distinctions between each, noting that the stronger the basis of power, the greater the power. They also defined power in terms of "influence, and influence in terms of psychological change",[27] which is important if one considers influence as a verb instead of a noun. French and Raven consider psychological change to include changes in "behavior, opinions, attitudes, goals, needs, values..."[28] This change may allow students and instructors to maintain a sense of purpose or confidence, one could surmise. Yet, it is the source of the power that is most revealing. If the power is personal (self-derived), as opposed to social (otherly derived), then one is capable of repeatedly influencing and impacting one's own personal landscape, enacting a psychological change that gives rise to a transformation in attitudes and values. It is this change that affords mature students the motivation to become authentic or true to self and succeed, and there is no indication that the power is dependent upon one's social or economic status. One could speculate that social power is fleeting for many students who hail from disadvantaged backgrounds. This is not to say that it is unwelcome or not viewed as beneficial, but rather, that it takes a subordinate position to the personal power. Many students seek a legitimate, expert, and/or referent power based on credentials they hope to work towards and obtain. However, personal power impinges upon social power.

Positionality, which Tisdell (1998) refers to as being self-determined based on several aspects of one's identity—including race, class, and gender—effects social standing "relative to the dominant culture."[29] Yet, in terms of motivation and authenticity, positionality may have less of an influence than the literature suggests. Students may express a hesitancy about moving forward with their college careers, particularly those who have been out of school for several years. Some may express a sense of low self-esteem, but these issues could be based on personal factors, and not necessarily on any perceived socio-economic standing. Yet, let us be clear. Our developmental students' socioeconomic status is the elephant in the room. Longitudinal data from multiple studies yet affirm the same sad reality: Our developmental education students tend to be overwhelmingly poor, of color, graduates of underperforming public schools, first-generation, and grossly underprepared for academic rigor. These demographics have changed very little over the last twenty-five years, although recent data by Chen & Simone (2016), among others, suggests developmental education placement is becoming increasingly more widespread and diverse, affecting disadvantaged and advantaged populations of students.

Knowing-in-action and reflection-in-action are two concepts espoused in the literature that address how authentic educators and their students may display a certain awareness or understanding while doing. This understanding becomes internalized; it may be acquired or performed in informal settings and, as such, may not be articulated or valued as a result. When students become cognizant of their decision-making and budgeting skills, per se, and begin to value these skills acquired when they had to think on their feet, this is what Schon refers to as "knowing-in-action."[30]

The authentic teacher, in an effort to foster authenticity in his or her students via an attitude of care, "engages with the larger questions of purpose in regard to education... conveys how the subject matter matters in the real world and possibly in her students' lives, (while) connecting learners in authentic conversations or dialogue around significant... issues in relation to the subject matter, and are guided more by caring for the education of students than by their own self-interest...."[31]

## Humor and Adult Learning

Although there is some evidence that humor is not always appreciated in the classroom as a "serious" pedagogical or andragogical tool, there is also compelling evidence that certain types of humor improve the learning experience for adult students. The key in terms of positive outcomes is in the type of humor utilized. Sarcasm and other "dark" forms of humor were roundly frowned upon in the literature, but "professors often used humor, students supported the use of humor, and both faculty and students favored the more positive types of humor."[32] Moreover, the effective use of humor in a classroom setting had several significant attributes related to student engagement. According to at least one study, humor "had the power to make teachers more likeable, facilitate understanding of course material, lower tension, boost student morale, and increase student attentiveness."[33] These are not outcomes to be lightly regarded, for when used appropriately, when it emanates from a genuine and authentic caring ethic, the humor alone has the power to transform lives. This may particularly be the case when one considers the psychological and emotional functioning of traditional-aged students, who often are most in need of reassurances and safe classroom spaces.

This notion is again supported by the literature. According to Carney-Crompton and Tan (2002), "traditional students exhibited poorer psychological functioning when they were less satisfied with their emotional support networks. In contrast, psychological functioning within the nontraditional students was independent of the amount and satisfaction with their emotional and instrumental social support resources."[34] This is quite conceivable, for psychological functioning, one could surmise, is itself one byproduct or overall measure of one's maturity and is quite irrespective of cognitive development.

Labouvie-Vief and Diehl (2000), in a study describing cognitive complexity and cognitive-affective integration, indicated that "age and education were significant predictors of the cognitive complexity factors...." They further posited the notion that a "qualitatively new form of thinking" could emerge in adulthood, and that this thinking would "involve a higher use of reflection and the integration of contextual, relativistic, and subjective knowledge."[35] Riegel (1973) referred to this as "dialectical thinking." Others (Baltes and Staudinger, 1993; King and Kitchener, 1994; Kramer and Woodruff, 1986) refer to the knowledge which emanates from this type of thinking as "wisdom-related" or "post-formal" knowledge, inferring that a degree of maturity and/or experience must accompany this development. This would be position nine, the last position in Perry's (1999) schema, and Belenky et al. (1986) refer to this as "constructed knowledge,"[36] the last position in their hierarchy of development.

Interestingly, it is the use of humor that complements this type of thinking, for humor was found to relax students and afforded the creation of a more reflective learning environment. This was found to be especially true for more abstract disciplines, such as statistics, or courses that students found to be either particularly difficult (and thus distasteful) or particularly laborious. Whatever the case, the utilization of effective humor in these courses was found to "facilitate the retention of novel information, increase learning speed, improve problem solving, relieve stress, reduce test anxiety, and (even) increase perceptions of teacher credibility."[37] In essence, humor, used in the right manner and certainly by the right individual, had significantly positive outcomes in terms of student success.

However, it is important to note that humor comes in various forms and not all "authentic" and caring instructors are able to utilize it effectively across learning venues. The effective use of humor is as much a function of personality and finesse as it is a pedagogical method. In the proper skilled hands, sarcasm could work in a learning environment as humor, yet in the wrong hands, the instructor could very well lose credibility and risk alienating him or herself from students and students from the subject matter.

The most popular types of humor for adults in a learning setting were narratives, comments, jokes, anecdotes, and the like. When students were asked to respond to a statement concerning a professor's use of humor as positive and con-structive, "79 percent selected always,"[38] although they also noted that perceptions of humor differed based on an instructor's gender; with a female instructor, humor might be overlooked, and other personal characteristics, such as race, ethnicity, or socioeconomic standing, were not factored into this equation. Overwhelmingly, students of one study indicated (at 97%) that they would also use humor in their own classrooms.[39] Interestingly, in this same study, sarcasm was listed as one of the top choices when students were asked what type of humor they would use in a classroom setting with adults.

Yet, the use of humor also was found to have its limitations, linking its potential ineffectiveness to the educator who does not come across as authentic or who lacks the skill and wisdom to utilize humor in adult learning settings as the art form it is. In the proper hands, humor in the context of a caring climate has the potential to yield powerful and lasting student overcomes. In the wrong hands, it has the opposite effect. No one can teach tact and diplomacy; the use of humor is all about the *how* of language use, and the *when* of timing.

## TRANSFORM Me: A Caring Attitude

It is no surprise that the role of faculty, administration, and staff is viewed as a facilitating factor in the development of students at most colleges. The issue is not merely one of a shared culture, faith, ethnicity, or community, but rather a climate of caring and a sense of how certain mature students are able to create more meaningful relationships with faculty that enable them to develop the competencies they need, regardless of compressed time. It is this type of focused engagement and attitude that educators across the board want to replicate.

For example, this caring attitude is embraced at a small southern university because it is taught and expected. Known for its "keen sense of community," the University requires all of their students "across all disciplines to have some kind of significant cross-cultural experience. (As a result), students end up teaching in Ghana, Greece, China, Vietnam, and a host of other far flung places."[40] What is instilled in students, this researcher surmises, is an *attitude* that facilitates in the development of needed competencies by even younger, traditional students. It also creates a campus culture, and since leadership and culture are connected, some theorize this mature, caring attitude must begin with and be seen in practice by college presidents and higher-level administrators. The fostering of this attitude, along with caring and committed faculty who are accessible and available, enables certain students to succeed.

## The Primacy of Noncognitive Competencies in the Context of Adult Learning

For years, research has suggested that in addition to academic knowledge, a variety of non-cognitive skills are essential to students' post-secondary success. These non-cognitive skills, attitudes, experiences, and behaviors are mindsets often studied as predictors of academic success. Research also suggests that when these skills and mindsets are in place, they are equal to or even surpass typical indicators of post-secondary success, such as grade point averages, test scores, and class ranking. They are primary, yet how do we tap into these skills and address them in the classroom? What is the correlation between the non-cognitive and pure cognitive ability?

Although not conclusive, the following mindsets or attitudes are often cited through research as top predictors of adult student success in the classroom and serve as the focus of this work:

1. Self-efficacy
2. Resilience
3. Self-determination
4. Responsibility
5. Motivation
6. Empathy
7. Agency
8. Perseverance

Moreover, there are certain success factors that can only be exemplified by faculty and the institution, including our expected academic norms and a climate of civility. Some of our students may not understand academic norms or academic discourse. Although debatable, a faculty member's speech, dress, comportment, etc., all cumulatively and unobtrusively address the expected norms of classroom civility, decorum, tolerance, and respect for differing perspectives.

# Part II – The Basement

## UNDERSTAND Me: Know Who You Are; Position Yourself to Know Your Students

In my early twenties, after receiving my undergraduate degree, I worked a number of jobs without having a true career. I had to find my passion. So I taught and worked in retail. I worked in insurance. I taught some more. I met all types of people in all sorts of employment situations. I saw the best and worst in human endeavors, and it allowed me to determine how and why work had to be relevant. There had to be meaning and significance at the end of the day. I realized soon enough that educating was not an option; it was the most liberating form of work to be had. From my perspective, the classroom had the potential to become that place of wonder, where radical transformation was not only possible but, in the right hands, quite probable.

I chose a community college in the Bronx, and they chose me. I worked on a dissertation during the evenings, and I taught my students during the day. They rushed away in the cold and rain before and after class, waiting for a bus or a train to drop them off downtown or across town in another borough. My babies, I called them, even though many were my age and even older were the ones who chose to stay close to home or the ones who had no option but to stay close to home, as well as those failed by a public or private school system that had systematically pushed them out, yet labeled then as dropouts or graduated them as college-ready when they couldn't express themselves in a coherent paragraph.

They were my students, and I claimed them: the working poor who were born in this country, as well as the immigrants who didn't speak English until a few months after they had arrived in lower Manhattan—penniless, clutching the address of a distant uncle who had kissed the ground when he arrived, and wrote home painting America as the land of promise, that is, until the uncle discovered he was summarily dismissed from even the consideration of jobs he was clearly overqualified for at home.

They learned informal English in days and weeks, while some native speakers chided them for their alleged "ignorance" and broken grammar. They drove taxicabs all night long and then arrived in my 8 am English class to challenge me, love me, and resent me, all at once. When they'd nod off, sometimes mid-sentence, chin resting on a palm, softly breathing, I'd gently tap on the edge of their desk. "Yes, mommy!" the men would jump upright in their seats, like tin soldiers.

They were mothers, piecing together two and three jobs all over New York City, raising their own babies during evenings and weekends and privileged babies each weekday. They took classes when they could, doing whatever it took—arriving in class with shades on to cover a black eye, or stealing a runny-nosed child into class and attempting to hide him behind their desk, under a coat, with a bag of potato chips to pacify, because they couldn't afford a babysitter. It was against College policy, and they knew it, but we both looked the other way, because we both understood.

## The Community College Challenge and Opportunity

As open access institutions, community colleges tend to attract as diverse a student population as one can find in any civic entity. Many are nontraditional adult students who have delayed their enrollment into college just after high school, or they may have had life to interrupt their matriculation plans for them. Yet, there is no doubt that these mature students "…face additional challenges to educational success because they are more likely to work full-time and may have families to support—characteristics that have been found to be significant barriers to educational success."[41] And it is not surprising that graduation rates are low, with more than half who matriculate at a community college leaving without a credential. Yet another large percentage go on to transfer and continue higher education at a four-year institution, which is our version of success. So many more are strivers, with stories untold. Our work is never facile or linear. As such, community colleges were so very worthy of President Obama's acclaim and commitment, for we annually educate and train more than 6.2 million students, nearly half of all undergraduate students in this country. For the committed, the work can be intense, requiring tenacity, creativity, and resources that often exceed availability and expectations.

Whatever it took to eke out a modest living my students were willing to do…to carve out for themselves a respectful place in society, to forge their own way to independence, to secure the pride that came with the ability to pay bills on time, and the respite that came in knowing they could feed their children without depending on charity. They did whatever it took to secure their vision of the American dream. They struggled for self-assurance in the midst of personal dissonance or cultural ambiguity. They did it every day, through economic recession, personal depression...whatever it took. And they taught me in ways I'll never forget, doing whatever it took to reach that next rung, even if sleeping in the college parking lot or a homeless tent city, or secretly washing themselves in the ladies' room basin the next morning.

Since the establishment of the very first community college in this country in 1901, we have, more or less, promised to be all things to all people. Community colleges exist to serve the community, and enrollment is open to all. However, what this means is that we have multiple missions in serving as the bridge to higher education for a very diverse student demographic. One of our primary challenges has been and continues to be meeting the needs of those who are the least prepared for college. Data from the American Association of Community Colleges indicate that nearly 60% of those who do matriculate at a community college come to us underprepared for college coursework and must, therefore, enroll in developmental (remedial) courses before they can even begin college-credit coursework. As a result, community colleges are spending an average of $2 billion per year on this one effort alone, while we continue to innovate, develop, and implement programs designed to meet the needs of all our students. We promise access, affordability, transferability, workforce development, credentials, remediation for what one did not acquire in elementary and high school, and more. Arguably, no other American institution in the public arena has ever promised to deliver so much with so little.

Community college faculty and staff are asked to perform what some scholars describe as a style of "democratizing magic" that largely goes unseen and unsung. This is nothing new. We have accepted that challenge for years, but in recent years, with more potential threats than ever imagined, colleges and students have reached the tipping point. As community college advocate and educator John Roueche aptly concluded over forty years ago, and the thought still resonates today: "Effectively serving the nontraditional student requires much more than the simple willingness to accept him." And yet, as we blindly leap into another decade of unparalleled economic inequity and uncertainty, many of our students worry and wonder if even the ideological willingness to accept them, where they are, still exists.

We are then compelled to ask:

Who are my students?

What do they say about themselves?

What do they believe about themselves?

What do they value?

Why are they in this developmental class at this point in time?

What do they even know about this class?

What motivates them? What captures them?

Where are they on the following "community-of-support" spectrum?

**Student Success (from less to most likely)**

| Tier 1 |
| --- |
| Totally Dependent on Others; Few Social Connections |
| **Tier 2** |
| Primarily Supported by Others with Limited Independence/Few Connections |
| **Tier 3** |
| Conditional Independence based on Agency Supports |
| **Tier 4** |
| Independent, Fragile Worker; Marginally or Wholly Connected to Community |
| **Tier 5** |
| Self-Supporting with Significant Others and Community Connections |

Often, where a student lands on the spectrum, or what he/she self-discloses in regard to familial and social support, may serve as a more accurate barometer of their success potential than more traditional measures.

As such, it is completely misguided to insist, as some adult educators naively do, that "keeping" adult developmental students in the classroom and on the roster, is simply an internal matter of instructor charisma or methodology. While both are factors, the truth of the matter is, despite their motivation, drive, and resilience, many of the most sincere developmental education students attend class erratically, or are absent for long stretches of time, due to the very same complexity of environmental and structural conditions that held them captive as children and teens, leading to their lack of basic skill acquisition in the first place. They have survived for much of their life on little to no rudimentary life support, with insecurities of all sorts as daily constants (whole foods, transportation, housing, etc.), and they have managed this way for years. Impermanence becomes a lifestyle. Some bounce from one relative's couch to another, or from one foster home to another. They may be the first in a multi-generational family line to attempt college, or even graduate from high school. As a result, they may have no role models or life coaches, and any discussion of their post-secondary life experiences become a foreign language to friends and family. They exist on a diet from the "dollar menu." They are ashamed of this and will not describe their daily struggle. They will, in fact, swear to the contrary—even when they are on the brink of disaster.

## Faculty: Show up Prepared and On Time

For many developmental students, you as faculty are the only role model they will see. You are the standard-bearer. If you are absent from class, they may very well regress to detrimental, yet convenient patterns of behavior and thinking, whereby attendance in class was simply not important or optional. Many of them are in their current state of academic lack or have serious gaps in their learning, because they were not in class to acquire foundational skills. If this attendance-as-optional mindset is not broken early, later scaffolding of knowledge and skills becomes nearly impossible. The student becomes frustrated, discouraged, embarrassed, and checks out first emotionally, then physically, or both simultaneously.

The first few weeks are critical. This is where you set the tone. This is when something akin to the beloved community could be realized. It is called the learning community, of course, and yet its essentiality rests on the same foundation. In this case, classroom standards of acceptability become normalized. Since you are at this point the sage on the stage and all eyes are rightly upon you, a routine can be established.

Essentially, how did your students get here, and how can you lift them to get there? The following understandings and attitudes are essential and foundational. This is the basement.

1.  Professional Comportment – They must know that you are serious, and this classroom is a place where learning is taken seriously. Command the classroom! If you're standing before them daily in jeans, using colloquial English, and obviously unprepared, this is less likely to happen. They will mimic your behavior, which is a recipe for failure.

2.  Humility – Teaching and learning are transactional processes. Your students should understand that you value their narrative. "Tell me your story so I can learn from you, just as you learn from me."

3.  Accessibility – Access, professional boundaries, and formal manners are thin lines to manage, driven as much by professional preference and etiquette as by personality. You do want to let your students know who you are, and what you have accomplished (endured) to have the privilege of standing before them as a professor. They should understand that if you are referenced as "Dr. Smith", you have earned that title and credential. Unless

the degree was procured through a diploma-mill type institution, it has cost you something beyond the mere monetary expense, and students should know this. It was not gratuitous. A price was paid. Thus, if you ask students to address you by your title, they should certainly honor that request. Some educators, appalled by the informality driven by social media, insist upon formality as they would insist upon good pedagogy. We must teach our students what they do not know.

One of my African American colleagues told me he insists his students address him by the formal title of "Dr. Smith," because too many of our ancestors were denied the opportunity of higher education. Many violently lost their lives simply by attempting to learn to read. In 2015, African Americans earned only 6.5 percent of all doctoral degrees awarded to students who are U.S. citizens or permanent residents of this country[42] and, for many of us, the use of this earned title enforces not only professional boundaries, but egalitarianism, and mutual respect, while countering a casual sense of student entitlement.

However, formality in the use of titles should never be confused as the gauge of one's respect amongst students or colleagues. Respect is an earned distinction. You cannot force it through the use of a title. One does not influence the other. Most of my students know I care about them, but this relationship guides the respect factor and takes precedence over a title.

Often, former students, whom I may have failed, will see me in the college corridors, smile, and speak to me still, asking me how I'm doing—not because of a title, but because of my approach to them. Because of my culture, and the community from which I hail, I may allow my students—who often hail from a similar culture—to address me as "Dr. Pamela" or even "Miss" because I understand the latter designation of honor.

4. Personally, I do not encourage faculty to be on a first name basis with students or provide students with their personal cell phone numbers. Too much familiarity can actually negate the very civil climate you want to establish in the classroom. We are not best friends with our students. I am cordial with all of my students, but I am not collegial. My intent is not to befriend; my intent is to inspire them to get to the next level.

5. Acknowledgement of Structural Limitations—
   You can only do in the classroom what institutional culture/politics/policies will allow and dictate. Your performance can never be based on you alone.

## PERSUADE Me

Many of our students are one car repair or babysitter mishap away from withdrawal—formal, mental, or otherwise. Even the most resourceful and resilient will fall by the wayside without an occasional helping hand. This "help" could be as simple as a word of encouragement. We all may have stories of the single parent-student who worked two to three jobs while managing a family and attending college in the evening, ultimately making it into his or her desired program by sheer grit, but having to withdraw in order to work and support a family because child support payments suddenly stopped coming in, and he/she had no other human or monetary resources in the world.

I have been an administrator and English professor for many years, teaching courses from Advanced Placement Language and Literature and Honors English, to World Literature and Critical Thought. I have taught high school students who would be considered educationally privileged, ranking as national merit honorees, to college students who rose from nothing and went on to become successful, productive members of their communities. I have also quite proudly served as an instructor of developmental English, and if you're one of my developmental students, there are two things I know about you:

1.  You're probably conflicted and confused because you have a high school diploma, and you were grateful to register for college classes, the first in your family to do so. You took a test, and the college took your hard-earned tuition dollars in return. But somewhere along the way, the college decided you weren't quite ready to take the courses you thought you'd take, the ones leading toward a degree, and this diminished you.

2.  You've made it this far in life by sheer determination and grit. You're hardly stupid. Some of you may have obtained high grade point averages in high school, or taken AP and honors courses. As a result, your frustration with this entire scenario has justifiably reached a boiling point. You may respond with anger, fear, resentment, self-pity, or all of the above.

Yet, this is what you must know. The *how* of your being in a developmental class in college is not easily answered, primarily because there is no standardized data specific to remedial or developmental education at the national level.[43] At some colleges, enrollment may simply be a matter of where you score on the required placement exam in English or math. But, as a high school graduate, how did you fail to score adequately on this most basic test? Even if English is not your primary language, or you've been out of school for many years, the test, most often the Accuplacer, evaluates your skills in math and English, or your readiness for college.

### "Miss, how do you talk like that?"

 The vast majority of the developmental students I teach are African American, Hispanic, second generation immigrants, and/or students who are financially insecure—the working poor. After rent is paid, they have very little left over. Conversely, when I teach honors students, regardless of where I teach them, they are overwhelmingly white, Asian, and/or socioeconomically affluent.

As adult educators, whether faculty or administrators, we are teaching students all of the time by example, and much of what we teach occurs when students are observing what we do, and listening to what we say. We are teaching concepts from our particular scholarly field, but we are also teaching "veritas," honor, responsibility, respectability, and on and on, whether we signed up for the job or not. Meaningful teaching occurs the moments before class, after class, in the office, and walking down the corridor. It occurs every time we see a student with his/her head down, or an overwhelmed expression on her face, and we make the decision to stop— in the midst of running to a meeting—and say hello, or ask, "Is everything OK today?" before listening for what is said, and then for what is not said. We must be fully invested in addressing their humanity before we can begin to address their cognitive development.

Walking down the corridor one day, I heard a familiar voice behind me. One of my female developmental English students was running to catch up with me. "Miss, miss," she yelled out, smiling and exuberant, and then shyly, once she caught up to me, "Miss, how do you talk like that?"

I stopped for a moment to fully absorb not only what she had stated literally, but her intent. She and her mother had immigrated to this country from Jamaica, with little more than the shirts on their backs, fleeing incessant poverty, and leaving all the love and family they knew behind. It was the sacrifice one mother willingly made to give her daughter the chance at a better life.

The 19-year-old student before me worked at McDonald's. Her communication skills were quite weak, yet her personality and spirit of resilience could capture anyone. She came to class in used, wrinkled clothes. Her hair was often unkempt, yet she knew enough about life in this country to intuit that individuals often judged her by her native patois, or inability to write and speak in standard English. It may have been an unfair assessment, but we all know this type of intellectual stereotyping occurs daily, on the spot, at first impression, as soon as one opens the mouth. There was not much she could immediately do to change her appearance and financial situation, but she knew she could learn.

I tilted my head and teasingly suggested that she just wanted to be a polyglot, switching linguistic gears when necessary "so you can impress everybody. I know you, Davida!" She smiled and laughed easily. I told her I was "extra" like that, too, and she looked me in the eyes, wondering and longing. "No, really Miss, how you talk like that?" Thus, the true teaching begins.

It's the real-life application of a concept that creates energy, engagement, and understanding for adult students, and particularly students of color, who will tell you they have absolutely no time to waste, even when they're feeling insecure about being in and belonging in college. Many will tell you they never thought about attending college, had put it off for years, and now find themselves trying to swim upstream alone. It is disconcerting, at best, and we will lose many if we cannot, or are unwilling to, embrace them into the community.

I have taught rhetorical and grammar concepts to adults using popular culture, and poetic elements using the genius lyricism of Tupac and Eminem—the cleaned-up versions. As stated previously, many colleagues utilize and create such strategies on-the-fly. It is intuited andragogy: We create and implement based on the immediate needs of the adult students right there before us, and assessment comes quickly via students' ability to confidently attempt the calculation, composition, or synthesis. Understanding is immediately recognizable and gauged based on students' own critical questioning. What some educators realize later is that, over time, researchers may conceive of a name for these techniques, although naming a technique, strategy, or style does not equate to discovery and ownership of it. This distinction is important.

# Part III – The Ground Floor

## ATTEND to Me

*It's 7:30 p.m. and this class doesn't end until 9:00. I'm tired and unfocused. It's not that I can't hear you. I'm not trying to be disrespectful when you ask me a question, and I just stare, but my family's about to be put out on the streets, and I need somebody to talk to.*

*I come here with a truth about myself. My dirty little secret is that I can barely understand this play I'm supposed to be reading and analyzing. I know that I've been what you call "underserved" by my public schools. Nobody ever took me under their wings or checked to see if I could read. But every day I manage to make my way through life, somehow, scared all the time because I can't understand the words on some of these forms I get, and I don't always know for sure what I'm signing. I'm ashamed to be found out. I can't help my ten-year-old with her homework, so when I make my way, it's kind of amazing. It's genius, really, if you ask me. I know how smart I am, because I'm twenty-eight years-old. I've been doing this since ninth grade—faking everybody out. I even made all B's in my high school English classes, and I made it through Algebra with C's, and liked it, too.*

*Consider my peers who were like me, who did not make it here this morning, who never will, because they don't even think about a better option, or maybe they are lost in another system, not a good one at all, or worse.*

*If I'm honest with myself, though, I'll confess that I can barely figure out these lines you just assigned us to read. I'm angry at you for giving it to me in the first place and "raising the bar" as you put it. But I'm mainly angry with myself. I cry myself to sleep so many nights, not knowing what to do or who to trust.*

*Right now, I think you really want to help me, and I think you probably can, but for me to be here, my ten-year-old is babysitting the three-year-old. There's no phone in the apartment, and I have the only cell. They slipped the orange piece of paper under my door last week, and I know it means we've got to go. We gotta move again. I know that much without even trying to pronounce everything on the paper and figure out words "in their context" like you say we should. Some things, I just know.*

*Like I know I need this class. I know I need a chance to be better, so I can take care of my children and create a future for them. If I'm ever to be a role model for my kids and make something out of my life, I need this, but can't afford childcare. Nobody in my family can help with all that I'm trying to do. They have their own problems. Everybody's just trying to make it, and nobody really understands this, anyway. So, I'm sitting here, trying to look "mentally engaged" as you say I should. Trying to be the intelligent young woman you tell me I am. But I argue with old people all day on my job and I come home and cook dinner, and sleep a few hours before I have to get back up again and come here, leaving my babies home alone. I'm worried out of my mind that they might set something on fire, and you want me to talk about Romeo and Juliet?*

How do I draw my students out?

What activities and strategies and attitudes will I use to build on and validate the non-cognitive strengths they already possess?

Successfully teaching developmental and gatekeeper courses, particularly to students who may lack confidence and support, is as much about science (understanding the research), as it is about art (instructor's personality and style). It entails a measure of both, the exact quantity to be determined by the singular needs and traits of any one class. The science is formal, as well as anecdotal. No one should discount or devalue his or her own hard-won classroom experiences. The art is knowing how much content to deliver, in what format, and when to stop delivery. It is to be quite intentional about our methods and strategies—on the fly intentional. It is about eye contact, precision with one's language, and the ability to pick up on non-verbal cues. Most importantly, though, it is the opportunity many of us miss: The art entails intuiting exact times when we are able to publicly acknowledge a student's non-cognitive expertise and skill, those "other" intelligences, unique life experiences, and the value of such expertise and experience.

As educators, we will discover that once adult students know we value them as whole individuals with untapped potential, they will work on projects all night long if necessary. They will rise to the occasion, going well beyond what is expected of them, because *you* believed they could meet certain standards, facilitated the process with your complete effort and skill, and expected nothing less. Quite often, we subconsciously ascribe value and respect to academic knowledge and skills alone, or we advantage this knowledge above the skills required to simply make it from one day to the next. Honor and acknowledge the latter, and you will astronomically impact the former.

---

One of my former students reached out to me via social media, years after I'd had her as a student. I immediately remembered her. She told me that I had "opened up the world" to her, a world she never even knew existed. I taught her Freshman Composition in a community college in the Bronx, and she told me she was working towards her master's degree now. I yet remember her moment of epiphany. As most of the class commiserated and sympathized with Othello's Desdemona, scanning the play's lines for evidence of her innocence, she looked up from her textbook, shook her head, and loudly proclaimed the woman was "stupid, just stupid!" I asked her to elaborate about it in a research essay. She did and wrote so passionately that upon sharing it with the class, the half-asleep, partially bored student in the back woke up.

---

## Where We Stand

Although each classroom varies, to address non-cognitive factors and build upon them, the guiding premise, strategies, attitudes, and cultural supplements that follow may prove to be helpful. It is worth noting here that most of these methods require one to extend himself far beyond the mere lecture-from-behind-a-desk format. They often require risk-taking (leveraged by professional discernment), authenticity, care, and a certain amount of transparency. One must be comfortable with the demonstration of all of those techniques to usefully employ them.

**Premise:** There is nothing new under the sun. What can and must we learn from those who have walked this road before? Every culture stands on the shoulders of its own giants who have paved the way for those to come.

## ENGAGE Me: General Strategies/Attitudes

1. Spend little time behind a desk or podium.

2. Circulate the classroom. Post affirmations! Speak affirmations!

3. If you are an administrator, take every opportunity to spend time in the cafeteria, library, at student club meetings, or wherever students can see and know you.

4. Make eye contact with students, regardless of their perceived ability to comprehend.

5. Model everything that you can in accessible language.

6. Read to them. Let them hear sarcasm, passion, indignant language, etc.

7. Talk with them, not at them.

8. Dissect every concept. Make it immediately relevant and applicable to their lives. To do this, you must know them. (I like to explain the thesis statement as the essay's GPS, or the car's engine.)

9. Provide "relevant" topics for students to write about and discuss.

10. Insist upon the risk-taking and then applaud the effort.

11. Question judiciously.

12. Counsel.

13. Mentor, even if it's just minutes before or after a class.

14. Demonstrate accessibility and a willingness to answer even the most basic or simplistic questions. If one has established a safe and respectful learning environment, students will ask just about anything.

15. Share the lived experiences of their elders, and your own. (See **Premise** above.) There is truly nothing new under the sun.

16. Supplement your instruction inside and outside of the classroom (videos, podcasts, documentaries, yourself, etc.).

**Cultural Theme:** Focus on the cyclical nature of oppression, struggle, labor, and survival as life paradigms.

**Cultural Supplement:** Focus on instrumental historical and popular culture icons.

**Younger faculty and administrators:** Begin early to amass a *repository* of "overcoming narratives" for diverse students of various abilities. Be prepared to counter every "I can't" with an "I can" narrative of that one who transcended his reality by transforming his perspective of reality.

See *Appendix, Student Voices, "...On Perseverance."*

# Eight Critical Competencies to Note

---

## Principle/Non-Cognitive Competency or Skill
## 1. Self-efficacy (personal power)

---

Self-efficacy is a higher-order concept that is displayed as confidence in one's ability to face challenges and affect situations. Self-efficacious students manifest a sense of belonging, even when the environment is foreign to them. They are confident they can get through a situation. This is difficult to express and believe when one is concerned about being evicted, concerned about a parent undergoing surgery, or how to feed children, and yet, they do. How do we, as educators, channel this obvious strength to build upon it?

### Strategies/Attitudes

a. Socratic Questioning

b. Despite the popularity of the flipped classroom, allow your struggling or overwhelmed students time to read, compose, calculate, and process in the classroom, with you. Let them hear you read passages aloud, with proper inflection and passion, and check for understanding with Socratic questioning. In this manner, the group responds, with you strategically facilitating (paraphrasing), so no one is embarrassed or made to feel uncomfortable.

### Cultural Supplements

a. Based on students' lived experiences (not your own), Socratic questioning is "generalizable" or a non-specific "personal", yet relevant. Is the exercise applicable? For example, ask "If you were required to write this report to your boss, would she understand it? Would she excuse or overlook your grammar? How important is it to communicate clearly at work? How many times do you want to read a memo? Does time matter?"

b.   Again, validate their perspectives, experiences, and what they already know as indispensable and foundational.

c.   Students develop agency, participation increases, and confidence in one's abilities multiplies when there is an awareness of personal metacognitive strengths. As such, this awareness should be explicitly taught to increase self-efficacy. Students who understand how they learn best can reflect upon these strengths, and consciously seek out learning modalities that work for them.

### Assessment Indicators

1.   Authentically ASK students how they feel in the course, at the college, etc. Provide journal topics that allow them to express how the institution might enhance their experience.

2.   Socratic questioning – Analyze their responses to discussion prompts. What's stated? What's NOT being stated? Broaden their thinking and perceiving with queries that force them to question their assumptions. Appropriate follow-up questions—to take home—extend the learning.

## Principle/Non-Cognitive Competency or Skill
## 2. Resiliency

Resilience may be considered a bi-product of self-efficacy. Resilient students appear to bounce back from adversity with greater facility than most, although one cannot discern internal dissonance or wounding. Yet, resilient individuals also tend to persist. They do not easily give up or give in; thus, understanding and cultivating these behaviors and beliefs can be valuable.

### Strategies/Attitudes

Do not weaken resilience by meeting their every need or lowering standards. If feasible, reinforce the reality that students can bounce back from that "D." Their ancestors did. Attitude is important here. As instructor, share your personal narrative of resilience in snippets. Help students to focus on today and where they are in the course, as opposed to where they've been. There should be no assumption that other options exist.

### Cultural Supplements

a.  Acknowledgement of our students' survival skills as "genius"—the fluidity of epistemological concepts in and outside of the classroom. Let your students know that for many collectivistic cultures, resilience has always been the driver. We do not stand alone, but we do stand on the shoulders of giants who refused to give in.

b.  Resilience, like resistance, can be taught if there is an understanding of it as a tool: a manageable, ancient survival tool that has been used for years. Discussion topics (even math problems) might focus on civil rights icons. Take every opportunity to recall iconic figures who stood firm (i.e. Mandela).

c.   Visuals also matter. Post or write clearly at the front of the classroom: Demographics is only destiny if you lie down and choose for it to be.

## Assessment Indicators

Recognize that students are overwhelmed with competing priorities and ask, genuinely, at the beginning of each class, "How are you? How is life treating you?" and then listen for what they say and what they do not say.

## Principle/Non-Cognitive Competency or Skill
## 3. Self-Determination

Self-determined students are self-possessed. They are autonomous; making decisions and choosing actions free of external pressures. These individuals do not readily follow the crowd. In a sense, they have learned to feel competent in their decision-making, which is not to say they are confident in the accuracy of their actions, but they have learned to trust themselves. These individuals tend to be self-efficacious and responsible, as well.

### Strategies/Attitudes

a.  Students need early success in order to set the stage for competence. A low-stakes initial assignment may be key here. We want to elicit confidence from a sense of competence.

b.  Recognition of the intersectionality of contemporary life, history, and cultural icons. Congressman and civil rights icon John Lewis recalls being beaten and left bloody by an angry mob in Mississippi. He tells how they (young SNCC members, many of them college students) didn't give in. "We kept our eyes on the prize," he told a commencement audience at Washington University. "And as students, as graduates, you must keep your eyes on the prize. You have a moral obligation, a mission, and a mandate..." What is meant here? Can you begin your class with a 5-minute reflection exercise? These students chose to do what they did, regardless of what the rest of the world thought.

c.  All students, but self-determined students in particular, need CLEAR, visual, actionable plans. These pathways leading to possible workforce credentials and careers must be explained to students early on in accessible language (language they understand). They should not need to second guess "what are my next steps". All courses leading to a degree or certificate (general education and required major courses) should be outlined step-by-step, semester-by-semester.

## Cultural Supplements

Find the strengths and push the bar as far as you can. If your students are persistent and resilience, how did they get to this point? Why not give up? Ask your students why they continued and what they learned.

## Assessment Indicators

Allow students time to reflect on their actions and responses. Any opportunity to express a process is an indicator of competency for the student. If the student can express self-determination in one area, or at one level, they are prepared to reach another.

# Principle/Non-Cognitive Competency or Skill
## 4. Responsibility

Responsible students are those who are willing to be accountable for something or to someone. They have a duty, and they are willing to accept this control they have for a person or thing, as well as the outcome, be it positive or negative. Responsible students do not readily assess blame elsewhere in situations for which they are ultimately responsible (and thus liable). These students often understand their own sense of agency and self-determination, although maturity impacts the latter.

### Strategies/Attitudes

Share your personal narrative, to the extent you are comfortable. Share that which is applicable. No over-sharing. At what point in time did you take responsibility for your own mess-ups, and yet, you are still here?

### Cultural Supplements

Know the value of your personal and familial trajectory—what have you learned and sacrificed in order to be here? What have others in your personal/familial/cultural sphere sacrificed to get you to this point? (Take the focus from self.) For what and to whom am I personally responsible, and thus accountable? The "nothing/no one" responses can become lessons unto themselves. Take every opportunity to engage, build upon, and create moments of epiphany. Such moments may entail modification to very strict curriculums.

### Assessment Indicators

Assess often via attendance, as well. Who's showing up to class? Responsible students will stay with you (or let you know why they can't).

Students "disappear" for any number of reasons that may have little or nothing to do with you or the course. Research adequately points to the typical culprits: lack of transportation, childcare, housing, finances to purchase books, or an illness, etc. However, we should never allow our students to simply go missing in action. An email or text message coming from you—their professor, advisor, dean, etc.—can make a world of difference.

## Principle/Non-Cognitive Competency or Skill
## 5. Motivation

Motivation is a powerful, internal desire or drive to do or accomplish something, and it is perhaps the strongest determinant of student success, although it is impossible to measure and often fluctuates based on personal variables.

### Strategies/Attitudes

a.  Use of personal anecdotes (at one time I was where you are or know of others who were)

b.  In the developmental classroom, technology can be friend or foe. Make it a friend. Use it as much as possible, while keeping social media at a distance.

c.  Maintain high academic standards. Do not deviate. Insist, in a caring, calm, yet confident manner that everyone can learn. Then, ensure you are available to students and assign appropriate exercises, so this is a reality. If students sense you are genuine and caring, what will happen is that adult students who have worked all day outside the college, will come to your course and work all evening just as hard, because they know you believe in them and expect a certain level of intellectual performance.

d.  Accelerate the learning based on power teaching. When a caring, safe, and authentic environment is created, students will rise to the occasion. Power teaching is that moment, space, or time in the class-room when teaching and learning are transactional. This is to say both instructor and the students engage in a form of shared understanding or revelation that has the potential to transform a life, even if the full manifestation of that transformation is years down the road.

## Cultural Supplements

a.  Give them choices from time to time, and solicit their feedback. Their casual feedback is a formative assessment tool; you can work on a method that is not working before you go too far with it. Listening to them also gives you a clear understanding of metacognitive strengths, and you want to focus on their strengths. You can build on these.

b.  Guide students in performing rigorous and relevant research around areas where there is familiarity and deep interest or significance for their life.

c.  Speak affirmatively over our unmotivated students!

## Assessment Indicators

I also query my students at the end of each semester and ask them to respond anonymously. Sometimes, the more thoughtful will even ask if they can take the questionnaire home so they can think about it. These frank, thoughtful assessments can prove to be invaluable to your instruction. Ask students what assignments worked for you, and which did not? Did you always feel comfortable? Why or why not?

It is important to note that your best (mature) students will openly provide useful feedback, should you ask them, and these are not the students posting on Rate My Professor. Generally, the immature (and occasionally vindictive) swarm to such sites, which can be useful in certain situations. However, you do not want to base your praxis on immature thought.

## Principle/Non-Cognitive Competency or Skill
## 6. Empathy

Empathetic students often possess strong interpersonal skills and demonstrate emotional intelligence because of their ability to understand and share the feelings of others.

### Strategies/Attitudes

As conscious, caring adult educators, we must understand that many developmental education students enter community colleges unmotivated because of extreme discouragement, if not outright depression. Demonstrate empathy and bring it out of others by making direct eye contact. This

a.   demonstrates my care for you, and

b.   my desire to "get through" to you.

Model empathy by working with students one-to-one as much as possible. When this is not possible, create ways to break down concepts "on-the-fly", based on what you know about the students. Always encourage: "You can do this; you know this." Begin each class by asking students how they are doing, and how their day is going, and then wait for them to respond. Authentically ask, and if you can't authentically ask, don't ask at all. Empathetic students will pick up on your inauthenticity.

A "safe, respectful" environment must be maintained. While professional comportment is important, this is not always easy when certain students are clearly disruptive to the learning environment; college policy (formal and informal) must allow for support.

### Cultural Supplements

a.   Establish early on a college and classroom culture that values and accommodates the culture and background of our students. Adults already understand this "culture of academic success" in the sense that they understand grades and hard work (although not all will value them). So, now we must integrate the two in order to elicit "high intellectual performance."

b.   A recent Harvard study demonstrated the clear correlation between academic success and spirituality for students of color. Align your adult students of color with faith institutions. Provide opportunities to develop relationships with faculty and staff across the board. Although adults may have a dearth of relationships, they may still suffer from "relationship poverty" (John Gomperts) of the sort that builds social capital.

### Assessment Indicators

1.   Teach them to value communication as a tool to convey thoughts and knowledge with anyone. Then challenge students to demonstrate this "polyglot" ability; describe a concept in standard English to a superior, and that same concept to a peer, whose linguistic style or origin is akin to your own.

2.   Reflection essay responses and group discussions allow adults to reframe thinking and entertain varying perspectives.

## Principle/Non-Cognitive Competency or Skill
## 7. Agency

For this work, agency refers to the capacity of an individual to make choices, apply judgments, act independently, or display specific behaviors. It is conscious awareness of one's power and ability to initiate and control one's actions (even in the face of external influence). It is a sense of ownership and control over one's behaviors. Students who demonstrate agency are often self-determined individuals who are willing to accept responsibility for their actions.

### Strategies/Attitudes

Acknowledge and validate them when they do something risky, such as reading a passage aloud, particularly when reading is a challenge. Students who display agency are motivated to excel because they can and they believe there's a reason for them to excel. They take ownership over their actions and want to take ownership of their learning. Allow it by providing opportunities for independent research, or partnerships within the college or outside of it (service learning, etc.). For this student to bloom, learning must be immediately applicable to life. These are often leaders, and their self-knowledge rubs off on other students.

The judicious use of Socratic questioning, and facilitation of the resultant discussions, is extremely useful for students who are already aware of their actions and consequences.

### Cultural Supplements

a.   Immediately and publicly thank them for the effort. Periodically, I may thank them in their native tongue – Gracias/Danke.

b.  Explicitly embed the concept of metacognitive knowledge and understanding in all instruction. It is empowering when students reflect upon how they learn, and are able to conclude that although they have more trouble learning A, they are geniuses in understanding B.

c.  Make this knowledge relevant! How do students survive every day? What tactical survival skills do they take for granted? There is self-awareness and there is power in the ability to name one's malady. Only then can one strategize to counter it.

d.  For these students, there must exist an external (beyond the college and themselves) impetus. There is a spring of hope into which they can tap on a daily basis. It may be familial. It may be spiritual. It may be the one relationship with a faculty or staff member who took the time to explain and affirm.

### Assessment Indicators

Reflection exercises that ask students to explain a process leading to an action are solid assessment tools.

## Principle/Non-Cognitive Competency or Skill
## 8. Perseverance (grit)

Perseverance is the ability to continually pursue a goal in the face of difficulty or challenges. Students who persevere to achieve goals are steadfast; they will continue in the face of failure or opposition. The key to ascertaining one's perseverance is to understand the nature of her motivation.

### Strategies/Attitudes

a.   Approachability/Relatability is the key.  There is no me/you, us/them in this classroom. Bridge the gap by telling them your story, at the level where you are comfortable, of course. If you went to graduate school "against the odds" or worked two jobs while managing a family or caring for elderly parents, tell them.

b.   Access to meaningful resources will inspire students to persevere. When possible, allow students to engage in projects, whereby their peers become resources. In groups, there is the opportunity to provide informal one-on-one remediation, tutoring, mentoring, and coaching.

### Cultural Supplements

a.   Whatever you have overcome, if struggle was the core and you are victorious, tell them, and watch the room grow quiet. All eyes will be fixated on you. Vulnerability is endearing.

b.   The value of your narrative/my understanding of its oppression, and what it has cost you. Unapologetically use texts that speak to your students' social/cultural awareness and experience.

c. When possible, attempt to match struggling students and low-income students with service learning opportunities in the community. Incorporate into your syllabus any opportunity to match students with community mentors and agencies. In essence, provide them with access to the same resources afforded students at more affluent institutions. (Innovation is the key. We can and must invest in low-cost, impactful interventions.)

d. Historical/cultural affirmations visibly in your classroom or other setting, but also in your speech, and in your curriculum. Students must be exposed to opposing viewpoints.

### Assessment Indicators

1. Assess formatively by circulating as you teach.

2. Look at your students and call them by name, asking if they understand.

3. Provide low-risk ways for your students to demonstrate understanding (what-ifs and case studies to which they can relate).

4. Ask if they are pushing to get to the next level. Provide journal topics whereby they have an opportunity to reflect upon and plan for where they would like to be in 10 years. Ask what is stopping them?

## Additional Engagement Strategies

These strategies and attitudes are particularly noteworthy in terms of assisting and encouraging traditionally under-served groups and students of color in higher education to reach their goals:

1.  As this work emphasizes, for many developmental students, an affirmation of their non-cognitive competencies and experiences is as important as the development of cognitive skills. Non-cognitive skills development and validation is often primary and foundational to the acquisition of more academic concepts. Such non-cognitive competencies are often perceived as survival skills and, as such, are devalued. However, this acquired knowledge and skill must be appreciated and recognized.

    Consider the following quote from educators Ravitch & Cortese (2009): "Learning experts have long recognized that the key to acquiring knowledge and mastering skills is to have a base of background knowledge… those who have knowledge get more knowledge, and those who have less, get less. Background knowledge allows one to acquire new knowledge, to read and comprehend new information, to navigate unfamiliar challenges, to make inferences, and to deduce solutions. Imagine having to play a game of chess without knowing how the pieces move… that is the level of puzzlement that people face when they lack background knowledge."[44]

There is nothing more important than an *anticipatory, positive* attitude by the instructor, as well as high academic standards and the consistent articulation of these standards. The expectation is that such standards can be met by every single student in that course.

2. Rigorous courses, higher-order thinking, and high standards must then become embedded into the culture of the institution and the system. This is the norm! Most remedial students can intuit when the curriculum has been "dumbed down" for them, particularly mature students. They never appreciate it, and respect is immediately lost. With traditional age students, this lost respect may translate into a number of self-defeating acts, including repeated absences, mental withdrawal, failure to invest, apathy, or complete lack of motivation.

3. "No one rises to low expectations." – Dr. Vincent Tinto

4. Accelerated, contextualized learning communities taught by faculty who mirror the population being taught or have overcome similar challenges work extremely well for certain collectivistic groups, such as many students of color.

5. The realm of the affective—instructor authenticity, transparency, and sense of care—is highly effective, but should only be explored by certain faculty who are open to this area.

6. Engagement of positive family influences and spiritual leaders—via orientations and cultural celebrations.

Surround the student in a circle of successful expectancy, and place him/her on a higher community-of-support spectrum tier. Adult students of color often have strong ties to their faith communities. As adult educators, it behooves us to tap into this rich asset and marshal the energy and faith of every local agency willing to invest the time and love.

Suppose...

# Part IV – The Upper Floors

## RESPECT Me: My Name is Resilience

Growing up in Gary, Indiana, my tight-knit, resourceful family was considered poor by contemporary measures, meaning we lacked quite a few of the material goods so many people believe are required for everyday wellness. And my mother struggled daily with chronic cash flow issues. She was a single parent in the sense that she had no earthly spouse who could contribute to the daily functioning of our home, yet she hardly parented single-handedly. She came from a large, extended family, and they lived in close proximity. As a result, she had more emotional, psychological and, to a limited extent, financial support than some two-parent households, while those unbroken homes, so to speak, felt complete enough to deny the "village" concept that helped me succeed.

I grew up raised by the village, and this was long before Hillary Clinton popularized and thus Americanized a longstanding African maxim, which frankly has existed in American culture since the Pilgrims landed on Plymouth Rock. It was the village that raised scholarship funds when I was only seventeen years-old and thrust me into another world. I was accepted into and my mother allowed me to enroll into an affluent boarding high school on Michigan's upper peninsula. I had never even ventured more than sixty miles from my hometown, but the village wanted better for me, although neither I nor they knew what that meant.

Overnight, it seemed, my world shifted. It was vastly different—not better, as the village had surmised it would be, just different. And I was firmly planted in it. Educator Stephen Brookfield calls such planting "cultural suicide," because it is a willful turning from our mother's reach, a shunning if you will, of the familiar. One finds himself caught in between two worlds—the familiar from which you can never escape even if you wanted to, and the better life into which you've been thrust. Only it's not better. And the grass is always greener elsewhere. I can recall horrifically confusing moments in boarding school when at least two of my presumably more advantaged peers tried to harm themselves following a visit from their parents or, conversely, following receipt of the cashmere sweater that arrived in the mail in lieu of the visit. I recall the midnights I spent in dialogue with the troubled daughter of a senator, vainly attempting to persuade her that it would not be "cool" to be dead, as she insisted it had to be, since at that point she would be in no position to know if it was cool or not.

Because I walked this tightrope of sorts from a young age, and grew accustomed to maneuvering dissimilar worlds with as much grace as I could finesse, my positioning as an adult educator is always consciously dualistic. I am above and I am below. I am to the right and I am to the left, and neither pole is to be shunned or resisted, in life, or in the classroom.

# Tough Love/Difficult Conversations

Every student deserves to know his or her status in any course. Students and often, their parents have a multitude of reasons for taking any one course. Faculty would concede that students are there to pass the course. Regardless of whether they need the course to fulfill general education requirements, or as a facet of their major requirements, most students want and expect to pass the course. A few do enroll as lifelong learners, wanting the course content as personal development. These students are there to learn; this is primary and the grade is secondary. Since these students are often in the minority, it is important to understand that grades can serve as both motivating and punitive tools. They can make someone's day, or catapult another into despair and depression. Since we do not know the personal weight of a grade to the student unless the student reveals this, we must handle the business of grading delicately, sensitively, and with a thoughtful hand. We certainly assess based on the student's output and ability to produce clearly articulated learning objectives. Informal, formative assessments may be in order, and if so, this is where authenticity becomes paramount in the relationship.

As open access institutions, community colleges open their doors for all, regardless of student ability. For course placement, and other purposes unrelated to acceptance, they may request and utilize standardized test scores, secondary school GPA, etc. Unfortunately, placement tests, high school grades, and other such measures do not always reveal true capacity. Scores are manipulated, parents and guardians are insistent, and compassion reigns—as it should for overwhelmed admissions counselors. What this means is a student with very limited English skills, who should reasonably be placed in a course for English Language Learners where she can succeed at her own pace, may be inadvertently placed in a course above her abilities. Or a charming student who is somewhere on the autism spectrum enrolls for courses when the parents want their adult progeny to attain social skills, have a daily structure afforded other adults, or simply an educational chance in life. The professor may have no idea as to what to do to help, other than pass the student because of empathy, or fail this student who cannot perform along with the rest of the students and according to standard outcomes. In each case, a difficult yet realistic and humane conversation should be held quickly, well before the mid-point in the semester.

In each case, we should be very clear about expectations. If it appears the student will not be able to meet the stated learning outcomes as plainly noted on your syllabus, the student and all involved must consider what is a priority for the student: to pass the course, or to learn, or both? And then, what is conceivable? During a conference, I once had a mature student thank me after noting her limited performance. I'd asked what she understood and reviewed her strengths and areas of deficiency. Obviously, this had not been done often for this particular student. While we must be careful not to discourage anyone, transparency is key, as resources are limited. Ultimately, she decided that she wanted to stay in the course because she was learning, even if it meant failing and repeating the course but, due to financial aid guidelines, she could not afford to receive a grade that would compromise her GPA, so she later withdrew.

I have had similar conversations with my most academically neediest students who decide to take a week's vacation in the middle of the semester, determining that a week or two away for any reason will not impact their grade. Again, the focus is on grades instead of learning. Thus, many will return to college and the course, unable to recover. Such students want *you* to take responsibility for their lack of accountability. No one benefits when this occurs.

## Grade Inflation: See No Evil, Hear No Evil, Speak No Evil

The well-worn phrase is a humorous depiction of how many, if not most, adult educators tackle this thorny issue of grade inflation. We don't tackle it. In fact, we don't talk about it at all. We all know that it happens. We may even be partakers of it and understand how widespread is the issue, yet silence is the norm. Our silence is more than mere harmless complicity. Lifestyles, family standards of living, and future livelihoods may be at stake. I have heard high school teachers justify passing a certain student because they believed in him, which is to say they intentionally sent a student to college unprepared for the rigors of higher education because it was the easy thing to do. Perhaps they were able to painlessly assuage their own guilt while simultaneously bolstering graduation requirements for the institution.

My challenge for all such adult educators and administrators is clear. Query any major employer in your city or region. Pose this question: Since my institution has so many students who are apparently underserved by our current school systems and entering higher education grossly underprepared, and acknowledging that we *must* exist as an institution, would you object if we graduate our students still underprepared—by virtue of inflating their grades and thereby dishonestly representing their ability to perform certain skills—in order to send them to you as potential employees? In essence, would you be willing to lower your workplace standards if we lower our academic ones?

I cannot imagine any legitimate employer who would be willing to respond in the affirmative. And yet, when we issue our degrees, are we not assuring a certain basic skill set among our graduates? Even if graduates are able to obtain positions based on credentials alone, this is merely a foot in the door. They must produce if they are to stay. Increasingly, they are expected to think outside of the box and perform more complex reasoning skills. Yet, according to a 2011 report by educational researchers Richard Arum and Josipa Roksa, more than a third of all college graduates in this country demonstrate "no improvement in critical thinking, complex reasoning, and writing skills"[45] after having invested four years as undergraduates.

We can place the blame where we may. English professor William Pannapacker has much to say about that blame. According to Pannapacker, who has written under the pen name Thomas Benton, "a generational shift is taking place in which longer forms of writing are being replaced with shorter ones." The writing is much shorter prose—more memos and to-the-point, concise e-mails—yet more sustained in thought, with other forms of multitasking going on. And this is good, yet according to Pannapacker again, "A growing percentage of students are arriving at college without ever having written a research paper, read a novel, or taken an essay examination. And those students do not perceive that they have missed something in their education; after all, they have top grades." And this is the crux of the matter for so many students in general, but particularly our developmental education students. *Many are recent graduates, and a percentage have top grades.* Yet, they do not possess higher-order thinking skills, the skills that will allow them to compete in a global, STEMM[1]-oriented society. It is quite possible to graduate from high school, diploma in hand, and not possess the requisite foundational skills needed to function in society. This is higher education's dirty little secret: It is just as possible to graduate from college without these requisite skills.

Further, in the United States, arguably one of the richest nations in the world, we consistently lag behind at least nine other nations on international comparison tests. America's global competitiveness is already suffering as our best students have consistently ranked behind their peers abroad in nations such as Hong Kong, Switzerland, South Korea, Canada, and Japan and in fields as critical as math and science.

"While American students are spending endless hours preparing to take tests of their basic reading and math skills, their peers in high-performing nations are reading poetry and novels, conducting experiments in chemistry and physics, making music, and studying important historical issues. We are the ONLY leading industrialized nation that considers the mastery of BASIC skills to be the goal of K-12 education."[46] (even as so many of ours fall short even of this "mastery").

Moreover, increasing numbers of students are entering higher education not quite college-ready, although nearly four out of five have graduated from high school with grade point

---

[1] STEMM – Science, Technology, Engineering, Mathematics, and Medicine.

averages of 3.0 or higher.[47] A large percentage of these students are people of color. According to *Strong American Schools,* a group that advocates for making public school education more rigorous, "A national survey of 688 students (in remedial college courses) found more than half saying that in high school they were good students who worked hard and nearly always completed their assignments."[48] Their numbers are increasing and developmental education's effect on the individual student can be devastating, with pernicious ramifications for the American dream.

## Parameters Impacting Education in the Black Community: Excellence and Accountability

We all suffer when academic standards are compromised so blatantly. Yet, many students suffer more than others, remedial students in particular, and students of color perhaps the most. A 2016 report from the Center for American Progress details remedial education as the "systemic black hole"[49] for many African-Americans, who do not readily emerge from it. This we know: There are certain documented initiatives, attitudes, and strategies for the engagement of traditionally underserved groups in higher education. Many are used informally by conscientious adult educators throughout the world. However, formal scaling up would require not only financial resources, and institutional goodwill, but often legislative oversight.

## The Black-White Achievement Gap

When Harvard University launched its Achievement Gap Initiative in 2005, they were looking at the educational disparities that exist between blacks and white students primarily, which can be seen across socio-economical lines, as reflected in standardized test scores and high school and college dropout rates. Of course, the so-called "achievement gap" has been studied for years and educational policy has been revised to address the issue. Educators around the country will speak of it and public-school superintendents everywhere have made various attempts to address it. Bill Gates has placed money around this issue. The Carnegie Foundation has supported research around "the gap," and think tanks of scholarship have studied the matter, but very little changes. The reality is that black and brown children still lag behind their white peers in nearly every educational variable measured via standardized testing regardless of socio-economical standing.

Our black and brown children are in crisis even before they begin to live. If left unchecked, the gap extends to higher education, where many adult students of color are left adrift, without positive faculty and staff of color to serve as mentors and role models. Many are left in an academic quagmire, without a clear and realistic pathway of required courses that will lead to particular majors and ultimately graduation. There is often a huge discrepancy between what students say they want to achieve professionally and, the finances, and education required to attain such a lifestyle. No one has taught them.

The issue is particularly acute for black men, who fall on the lowest rung of achievement in higher education. Yet, the realm of the affective can be a useful starting point when considering the education of males at an early age. According to Tyrone Bledsoe, executive director of the Student African American Brotherhood, "A lot of these young men have been disappointed so regularly that they don't trust and believe in anything. These young men want to be loved. They want to be cared for and cared about."[50]

We also know that a culture shift is in order. The emphasis on improving academic outcomes for students of color, and black men in particular, will occur when the will exists. This may very well entail a reallocation of funding and processes. It will also entail a network of support and commitment of organizations strictly interested in serving black men, as My Brother's Keeper and the Schott Foundation. We must also include the community of faith, as a resource and a strategy. The emphasis of spirituality is tremendously important in the lives of students of color, according to a 2017 Harvard University study. According to the report, "Populations at risk of adverse academic outcomes, especially black and Latino students, tend to have strong ties to faith communities."[51] This bridge between school and faith is an untapped resource not only for youth, but for the adults they become. If faith leaders are already providing "stability, support, and guidance to millions of young people in the United States," how might higher education leaders leverage this support for adult students of color by partnering with communities of faith in an effort to collectively and positively impact outcomes?

The report *Academically Adrift* pessimistically proclaims that an improvement in undergraduate education is unlikely to occur unless there is a huge culture shift in organizations. Change will not occur unless it is forced, and unfortunately this has huge implications for adult students of color. Arum and Roksa's position is that we must make "rigorous and high-quality educational experiences a moral imperative" for all.[52]

One might argue that not every student will go on to matriculate in college or even a trade school. This is certainly true. Yet, they will go on somewhere and to something. There isn't a single occupation providing livable wages that does not require basic literacy skills, and these fields are limited and diminishing due to technological advances requiring higher-order skills. The military, once a bastion of upward mobility for men of color who were not interested in college but wanted to establish themselves, still requires the equivalent of a high school diploma for enlistment. Still, higher educational demands are tied to many further promotions.

Additionally, our students are not necessarily competing with one another for jobs and careers, or even with Silicon Valley. Rather, they are walking into a workforce that is internationally competitive, where a multiplicity of intelligences—including a knowledge of STEMM concepts and basic coding principles, written and oral communications expertise, and interpersonal dexterity—is an imperative, or obsolescence is nearly guaranteed. A 2017 Department of Education briefing aptly warns of the United States' lagging educational achievement for its students in general: "On the Programme for International Student Assessment (PISA), a test given every three years to 15-year-olds in dozens of leading nations, American students essentially stagnated in 2012, while students in many other countries moved ahead. In the three years since 2009, the U.S.'s international ranking in math fell from 25th to 27th. In science, it slipped from 17th to 20th. And in reading, it dropped from 14th to 17th."[53]

The truth of the matter is, we really do know how to educate; we do know how to help students succeed. There is a body of literature concerning what works to improve student retention across the board. Aside from genuine care between instructor and student, young black men should be encouraged to read consistently, and challenged by rigorous courses and high expectations in a positive educational setting that aligns with students' major interests and professional goals. "No one rises to low expectations," educator Vincent Tinto noted, and this remains true. *"Nothing is more important than the consistent articulation of high expectations."*

According to John Jackson, president of the Schott Foundation for Public education, "the biggest race-linked gaps in achievement are in states with large black populations concentrated in schools with inadequate resources, poor teachers, and low expectations for their students."

Higher education leaders can counter this reality by preparing for engaged instructors, tutors, mentors, and community leaders who mirror the target population, or at least have overcome similar challenges. Moreover, to counter non-cognitive deficiencies, it is also beneficial to teach young black men how to master the principles of entrepreneurship, communications, finance, and business management. This education of the whole person creates a sense of confidence that will serve as a springboard for future academic challenges. As a final thought, Innovation is, and always has been, the key. We can and must invest in less-costly, high-impact interventions. It is a matter of budget reprioritizing, of course, and wise implementation of strategies by college presidents who determine to make true equity *the* pathway to student success.

## Final Implications

Critical to implementation of any success strategy is the collegial climate that should exist within the institution. Although the concept of the beloved community may seem anachronistic to some, the ideologically diverse and tolerant community can and must be realized through all means possible. This work has covered limited ground in terms of community building, yet there are noted hindrances that continue to distract, and we must continue to overcome them.

Hindrances to community-building imperatives:

1. Internal politics/sabotaging
2. Micro-aggressions and other covert inequities
3. Erasure of educators who affirm an equity agenda

On the other hand, community building begins in the individual course, with the individual instructor. As content experts, not all will have the desire to construct community, capture the heart of adult learners, or do the work necessary to ensure all students thrive. Such educators will view this additional cost as an infringement upon their personal time and space. They have every right to think this way, and can hopefully steer clear of higher education's most vulnerable populations.

In CAPTURING the heart of adult developmental students, and all adult learners in general, we affirm not only their humanity and potential, but our own. Our integrity as adult educators, particularly in community colleges, rests upon the charge to educate all who come before us. We are able to educate the souls of our students—the whole human being—

by meeting them where they are in life, and entering into their worlds, wanting to understand their strengths and gifts as foundational sources of power.

Care about them.
Attend to them.
Persuade them.
Transform them.
Understand them.
Respect them.
Engage them.

Capture their hearts—their faith in you, themselves, the world, and this unknown space of academia. You are then in a position to educate their souls. In so doing, you unlock the potential in adult learners to turn the world upside down, one individual at a time, family by family, and community by community.

How does this translate into real-world skills, jobs, and my quality of life?

What does this look like in, and more importantly, outside of the classroom?

# Appendix

## CALC: Contextualized Adult Learning Communities Model

### Park Your Ego at the Door

Contextualization is a constructivist approach to teaching and learning that continues to have important implications for adult educators, as this theoretical base assumes the <u>substantial</u> influence of culture, environment, family, and social relationships upon the adult learner and his or her ability to acquire and synthesize information. The contextualized adult learning communities (CALC) described in this manual are intended as year-long (fall, spring, and summer semester), thematically and culturally centered *villages* of internal and external constituents committed to wholistic student success. Each annual cohort will engage students from the basic developmental tier (English or math) through the next two tiers (semesters) of the discipline in a sequential fashion, with the same instructor(s). Research suggests "this approach may... increase in efficacy when institutions ensure that students enroll in corresponding college-level courses *as soon as they finish* their developmental counterparts. This sequencing of courses will help limit course avoidance and other barriers to college completion."[54]

Contextualized instruction for these particular learning communities is not intended to infer alignment of content with the student's major, but alignment of content with the mature student's life and adult responsibilities. The signature tenet of each CALC will be the fluidity or adaptability of curriculum delivery and methods based on students' needs *and* strengths. We are cognizant of the dynamic and evolving nature of communities and the role of the affective in methodology. As such, CALC's instructional methods will never be linear or identical from one cohort to the next.

Regardless of focus or theme, the following foundational precepts will guide in the development and implementation of CALCs:

1. The Contextualized Adult Learning Communities are inherently accelerated. Mandatory attendance is key, as supplemental instruction is *embedded* back into the course itself.

2. CALCs are as strategically incentivized as institutional and system-wide or state policy will allow. Incentives may be subsidized by the institution, or they may be grant funded. Prime possibilities include:

   a. monetary "rainy-day fund" based on attendance *and* performance;
   b. complementary textbooks and supplies, or the use of open educational resources (OERs); and
   c. tuition-free tier one course (the developmental tier).

3. Every facet of the three linked tiers is structured as a learning opportunity, rooted in adult learning theory

and/or practice. No time is wasted. The *context* is culture, life, and civic responsibility. Therefore, the first tier Developmental English (reading and writing) course may be appropriately taught in conjunction with a 1.5 or 3 credit First Year Experience course, offered jointly as one 4.5 or 6-credit developmental course. The objectives from both courses are converged into the one course, as students are taught basic principles of budgeting, compound interest, checking and savings, time management, academic research, etc. via readings, writing-intensive assignments and discussions that are immediately applicable to the lives of adult students. These FYE objectives may not be suitable or required for any math CALCs.

4. Due to the self-motivation, maturity, and accountability required of students for successful completion, students must apply to and be selected for the CALCs. Ideally, enrollment is capped, and students will be required to compose a brief, autobiographical letter of intent (LOI). An interview with potential students is optional; however, the LOI will enable the instructor(s) to initially structure the course with appropriate readings, assignments, and methods based on student interests, non-cognitive strengths, and expressed needs. Students must understand the expectations and benefits of the CALC at the onset. As such, full institutional support and compliance is necessary. How CALCs are marketed becomes critical to success.

5. Instructors and external village constituents, such as guest speakers and other community leaders and experts, should

in some fashion mirror the population being taught, hail from a similar background, have overcome similar obstacles, or empathize with the plight of underprepared and underrepresented students. For new faculty, these additional considerations may constitute a priority hire. Community is key, a caring ethic is key, and the CALC instructor, in particular, must be attentive and responsive to the dynamics of the group. Although boundaries will be established, instructors are expected to engage with students, in and outside of the classroom as advisors and mentors.

## Sample Year-long Structure for English and Math Sequences at Semester-based Institutions

**Fall Semester-tier I**
**Spring Semester-tier II**
**Summer Semester-tier III**
ENG 096/FYE    ENG 101/*FYE    ENG 102 (hybrid) and
MTH 095/SI    MTH 135/SI    MTH 137 (hybrid)

**Tier I** consists of a 3 to 6 credit course that links the developmental English course with the institutional objectives of a traditional First Year Experience course, or traits most noted by nontraditional adult students as life skills and abilities they "wish they had acquired" prior to graduating from high school. These include basic budgeting and finance skills, understanding of business documents such as leases, credit card usage and interest rates, basic computer skills, library and research instruction, etc., etc. The developmental Math course would not be required to link to the FYE course. Instead, computerized supplemental instruction, or some other form of SI, is necessary. For all CALCs, metacognition is explicitly taught.

**Tier II** builds on tier I and consists of the first semester, credit-bearing Composition or College Math course. Elements of the FYE course are embedded in the curriculum. Metacognition is explicitly taught.

**Tier III** is the second semester, credit-bearing English or Math course in the sequence. Ideally, this course is taught in the summer as a hybrid. This is to say that the first four weeks are taught on-ground and the second 4 weeks are taught online.

Student success is based on the clear understanding that for the duration of this year-long cohort, *the same instructor* is assigned to each tier course.

## Sample Lesson Outline

There is a plethora of technology in most college classrooms, including document cameras, computers, and other instruments. The use of technology is encouraged. When my students walk in the door, a journal topic and the day's agenda are already on the screen. Please note the basic samples below.

## Sample I - English 101

Journal Topic #8 – Pretend you are a Little League coach who is concerned about the poor sportsmanship demonstrated by the parents of some players. Write a brief letter to these parents that is intended to deter such behavior.

Agenda:

I. Journal Topic #8.

II. Module II – Analyzing Various Types of Texts
- HW was to read The Fashion Industry, p. 95
- How did the writer choose to analyze the two visual texts? What is her "evidence"?

- Notice her conclusion on p. 99. Do you agree? Did she prove her point? Is it effective?

III. TED Talk – David Epstein
  Questions 1 – 6 serve as our Discussion

IV. Analyzing Visual Texts

V. Independent Analysis p. 664

## Sample II - English 101

Journal Topic #9 – What individual, or individuals, do you most admire, and why? What traits do you most admire in this individual, and why?

Agenda:

I. Journal Topic #9

II. Module II – Analyzing Various Types of Texts
  - Review of Key Features
  - HW due today: *Just One More Game...* on p. 105. Please turn in your responses to analysis questions.

III. TED Talk:  David Epstein
  *Are Athletes Really Getting Faster, Better, Stronger?*
  (or is something else at play)
  - Analyze this talk by focusing on <u>his evidence</u>.
  - In groups, respond to the analysis questions posted.

IV. Visual Text Analysis
   - Choose ONE of the visual texts on pages 670, 677, or 688. Discuss and analyze with a partner.

V. Independent Assignment – *Well-Behaved Women Seldom Make History*, p. 664

Students know to come in and get busy. This is a safe space, but it is also a space where learning is taken seriously. Students are expected to come to class, to learn, and to produce. I demand it. Produce or stay home. The bar is high from day one. And yet, it must be if we are to be successful. We are sending students out into the world and the workplace; while it may temporarily alleviate personal guilt, or placate feelings to befriend them and send them forth with grades they have not earned, affirming knowledge and skills they do not possess, it is the coward's way and harms the student in the short and long-term. Most higher education professionals can readily name the one or two faculty members in the department infamous to their peers for passing every single student who comes their way with a "B" or above, yet beloved by students for this very same reason.

# Student Voices

The following section contains the words of anonymous students encountered in various development programs throughout the years.

## On Perseverance (student writer Stephen Sheak)

*"I had to persevere through every hurdle life threw my way. No matter how many times I fell victim, I got back up. Refusing to give up is what made me. In my world, it was always survival of the fittest, and I was rewarded beyond measure.*

*I found a higher power. I discovered that being at peace with yourself is greatly underrated. I'm able to rebuild my character. I have values, morals, principles, and self-esteem. I no longer compromise them for anyone or anything. I have real relationships, friends, family, and children. I am present for those that need me most. I am just so grateful to have a new perspective on life. All I had to do was change the way I looked at things and the things I looked at started to change (paraphrasing philosopher Wayne Dyer). So perseverance gave me a whole new life."*

## On Agency

*"If I could make one major change in the world, I would change the way people think about life. When I listen to the kids I went to school with, they have these viewpoints about the world that make me feel like an outcast sometimes. I mean, they are so negative, so down, I don't think they even realize how they sound sometimes.*

*I feel like an outcast because I've learned how to take charge of myself and my life. My friends, the people who live around me, their morals are far from positive. If I could just change the way they see the world, and the way they look at life in general, it might save a life. Really. If I could, I would show them how to be more positive and outgoing, rather than sitting around depressed, and full of self-loathing, or just angry at the world for no good reason. I feel this way because I have personally learned that if you will change the way you look at things, whatever you're looking at will change. Granted, certain things in life are just uncontrollable, but if you change yourself, and improve the way you look at life, life gets better. But if you think negatively, that negativity becomes your reality."*

## On Self-Determination

*"My parents never supported me because no one ever supported them. I was the first in my generation to attend college, and no one appreciated what I was trying to do. I carry the weight of the world on my shoulders because of that. I've never had a true support system my whole life, so I had to do things on my own. I was my own motivator and care-giver, and because I was paying for classes, books, and everything out of pocket, I had finances to worry about, and family issues that always seemed to choke the life out of me. But I kept going, even when I thought I really couldn't do it.*

*"I lost a lot of people along the way, just trying to get one degree. Every positive step or accomplishment I made meant that I lost somebody unwilling to accept that accomplishment and me as a package deal. But something within me wouldn't let me quit. It was like, I had come too far. So I pushed myself.*

*My electricity got cut off a few times, but I kept making A's, and my achievements were like a drug. I was high on making these grades because I had never been able to do that before."*

## On Self-Efficacy

*"My parents instilled in me certain values, and those values never left me. Even when I strayed away from them in the drug world, when I escaped that world, they were still with me. Narcotics Anonymous instilled and reinforced those same values in me that my parents had instilled in me as a child. So when I entered college many years later, I knew that I had to draw on those values, because they never left me. I knew what I had to do. I had to have a plan, and a part of my plan was not to fall into the negativity that others might bring. Some of my classmates try to talk to me about all kinds of foolishness, and disrupt my flow in the class, but I have goals that I need to attain. I've learned that you have to keep your eyes on the prize."*

## On Agency

*"To be focused and purposeful is necessary to succeed. I learn more and more about applying myself, and understanding that I'm more than worthy of spending the money I spend on books, more than worthy of putting the time aside that I need to put aside. I'm worthy of all these things, you see, and that's not a selfish place to be. It is all about understanding that I'm here for a reason. What I do here and now affects so many others in my family. So, if I'm not focused, I can't move in the divine space I want to move in."*

## On Empathy

"Faith is all I rely on, to understand myself and those around me. When my daughter was raped in 2003, in the middle of the semester, I wanted to curse God and die...but I still functioned. I still came to class, and I forced myself to communicate with people, because we all have hurts and disappointments. You must talk and share of yourself. It allows other people to feel comfortable with you.

"I know I don't always express myself well. I don't always know what word to use, or which word is correct, and I get embarrassed, thinking that I might make a mistake and have my intelligence challenged. But then I know that there are others who feel exactly the same way. People make these judgment calls all the time without even realizing that person might be tired, or sick, or just had some loved one taken away from them..."

## On Motivation

"In life, you learn how to do certain things because you have to. This is how you make it, and if you can't learn and learn quickly, then you slip up. It's not just about slipping up in your classes, but you're also slipping up in life when that happens. You know, if I can't read my bills or understand my lease, or some things that I sign for my kid at school, I could make a long-term mistake that might cost me and my child our lives, so I knew walking in, that I could do it, and that I would do it.

## On Self-Efficacy

"*One of my major drawbacks was my lack of under-standing of who I was and what I was capable of. When you lack self-awareness, you're vulnerable to other people's perceptions of who you are, even if that perception is completely wrong and detrimental to your health. It is who they need for you to be, and it can rob you if you don't know who you are.*"

## On Perseverance

"*I want to get my Ph.D. I don't plan on stopping until then, so I do whatever it takes to make it to class. It is not an option anymore. If I have to sit in that class and look up every word in the dictionary, I will do it. I'll do it because I know that I can, and I know that I must! At this point in my life, I know that I am a really deep thinker. I wouldn't have known that before, even though it was always there. I've always been intelligent, but I didn't know it. My environment wouldn't allow me to know it.*"

## Bibliography & References

[1] Chen, X. and Sean Simone. (2016). *Remedial Coursetaking at 2- and 4-Year Institutions.* National Center for Education Statistics. Washington, DC: U.S. Department of Education. Available at https://nces.ed.gov/pubs2016/2016405.pdf

[2] *Corequisite remediation: Spanning the completion divide (2016).* Indianapolis, IN: Complete College America. Available at www.completecollege.org/spanningthedivide/#home.

[3] Jimenez, L. et al. (2016). *Remedial Education: The Cost of Catching Up.* Washington, DC: Center for American Progress. Available at http://genprogress.org/wp-content/uploads/2016/09/30115238/CostOfCatchingUp2-report.pdf.

[4] Jimenez, L. et al. (2016). *Remedial Education: The Cost of Catching Up.* Washington, DC: Center for American Progress. Available at http://genprogress.org/wp-content/uploads/2016/09/30115238/CostOfCatchingUp2-report.pdf

[5] Mezirow, J. (2000). *An Epistemology of Transformative Learning.* Available at http://learningtheories.synthasite.com/resources/Mezirow_EpistemologyTLC.pdf

[6] Gutierrez, K. (2017). *Three Adult Learning Theories Every E-Learning Designer Must Know*. Science of Learning blog. USA: www.td.org/Publications/Blogs

[7] Gutierrez, K. (2017). *Three Adult Learning Theories Every E-Learning Designer Must Know*. Science of Learning blog. Available at USA: www.td.org/Publications/Blogs

[8] Caffarella, S. M. (1999). *Learning in Adulthood: A Comprehensive Guide*. New York: Wiley.

[9] Kreber, C. (2009). *Teaching and Learning within and beyond disciplinary boundaries*. New York: Routledge.

[10] Noddings, N. (2003). *Caring: A feminine approach to ethics and moral education* (2nd ed.). Berkeley: University of California Press.

[11] Smith, M. K. (2004). *Nel Noddings, the ethics of care and education*. The encyclopaedia of informal education. Available at http://infed.org/mobi/nel-noddings-the-ethics-of-care-and-education

[12] hooks, b. (2003). *Teaching community: A pedagogy of hope*. New York: Routledge.

[13] Kreber, C. (2009). *Teaching and Learning within and beyond disciplinary boundaries*. New York: Routledge.

[14] Kreber, C. (2009). *Teaching and Learning within and beyond disciplinary boundaries*. New York: Routledge.

[15] Kreber, C. (2009). *Teaching and Learning within and beyond disciplinary boundaries.* New York: Routledge.

[16] Taylor, C. (1991). *The ethics of authenticity.* Cambridge, MA: Harvard University Press.

[17] Kreber, C. (2009). *Teaching and Learning within and beyond disciplinary boundaries.* New York: Routledge.

[18] Jarvis, P. (1992). *The paradoxes of learning.* San Francisco: Jossey-Bass.

[19] Cranton, P. A., & Carusetta, E. (2004). *Perspectives on authenticity in teaching.* Adult Education Quarterly, 55(1), 5-22. Available at http://journals.sagepub.com/doi/abs/10.1177/07417136042 68894.

[20] Freire, P. (1971). *Pedagogy of the oppressed.* New York: Continuum.

[21] Collins, P. (2000). *Black feminist thought.* New York: Routledge.

[22] Belenky, M., Clinchy, B., Goldberger, N. & Tarule, J. (1986). *Women's ways of knowing.* New York: Basic Books.

[23] Knefelcamp, L. *Presentation comments, Psychology of Bigotry conference.*

[24] Perry, W. (1999). *Forms of ethical and intellectual development in the college years.* San Francisco: Jossey-Bass.

[25] Collins, P. (2000). *Black feminist thought.* New York: Routledge.

[26] Kegan, R. (1994). *In over our heads: The mental demands of modern life.* London: Harvard University Press.

[27] French, J. R. P., Jr., & Raven, B. (1959). *The bases of social power.* In D. Cartwright (Ed.), Studies in social power (pp. 150-167). Oxford, England: Univ. of Michigan Press. Available at https://www.researchgate.net/publication/215915730_The_bases_of_social_power.

[28] French, J. R. P., Jr., & Raven, B. (1959). *The bases of social power.* In D. Cartwright (Ed.), Studies in social power (pp. 150-167). Oxford, England: Univ. of Michigan Press. Available at https://www.researchgate.net/publication/215915730_The_bases_of_social_power.

[29] Tisdell, E. (1998). *Poststructural feminist pedagogies: The possibilities and limitations of feminist emancipatory adult learning theory and practice.* Adult Education Quarterly, 48(3), 139-157. Available at http://journals.sagepub.com/doi/abs/10.1177/074171369804800302.

[30] Schon, D. (1987). *Educating the reflective practitioner*. San Francisco: Jossey-Bass.

[31] Kreber, C. (2009). *Teaching and Learning within and beyond disciplinary boundaries.* New York: Routledge.

[32] Torok, S. et al. (2004) *Is Humor an Appreciated Teaching Tool? Perceptions of Professors' Teaching Styles and Use of Humor*, College Teaching, 52:1, 14-20. Available at https://eric.ed.gov/?id=EJ702016.

[33] Torok, S. et al. (2004) *Is Humor an Appreciated Teaching Tool? Perceptions of Professors' Teaching Styles and Use of Humor*, College Teaching, 52:1, 14-20. Available at https://eric.ed.gov/?id=EJ702016.

[34] Carney-Crompton, S. & Tan, J. (2002). *Support systems, psychological functioning,* and academic performance of nontraditional female students. Adult Education Quarterly, 52(2), 140-155. Available at https://eric.ed.gov/?id=EJ638697.

[35] Labouvie-Vief, G. & Diehl, M. (2000). *Cognitive complexity and cognitive-affective integration: related or separate domains of adult development?* Psychology and Aging, 15(3), 490-504. Available at https://www.researchgate.net/publication/12308443_Cognitive_complexity_and_cognitive-affective_integration_Related_or_separate_domains_of_adult_development.

[36] Belenky, M., Clinchy, B., Goldberger, N. & Tarule, J. (1986). *Women's ways of knowing.* New York: Basic Books.

[37] Torok, S. et al. (2004) *Is Humor an Appreciated Teaching Tool? Perceptions of Professors'*
*Teaching Styles and Use of Humor*, College Teaching, 52:1, 14-20. Available at https://eric.ed.gov/?id=EJ702016.

[38] Torok, S. et al. (2004) *Is Humor an Appreciated Teaching Tool? Perceptions of Professors'*
*Teaching Styles and Use of Humor*, College Teaching, 52:1, 14-20. Available at https://eric.ed.gov/?id=EJ702016.

[39] Torok, S. et al. (2004) *Is Humor an Appreciated Teaching Tool? Perceptions of Professors'*
*Teaching Styles and Use of Humor*, College Teaching, 52:1, 14-20. Available at https://eric.ed.gov/?id=EJ702016.

[40] McDonald, W., ed. (2002). *Creating Campus Community.* San Francisco: Jossey-Bass.

[41] Bailey, T. et al. (2005). *Graduation Rates, Student Goals, and Measuring Community College Effectiveness.* New York: Community College Research Center, Teachers College, Columbia University. Available at https://eric.ed.gov/?id=ED489098.

[42] *The Persisting Racial Gap in Doctoral Degree Awards.* (2017). The Journal of Blacks in Higher Education. Available at https://www.jbhe.com/2017/02/the-persisting-racial-gap-in-doctoral-degree-awards-2/

[43] *Developmental Education Challenges and Strategies for Reform.* (2017). Washington, DC: U.S. Department of Education. Available at https://www2.ed.gov/about/offices/list/opepd/education-strategies.pdf.

[44] Ravitch, D. and Antonia Cortese (2009). *Why We're Behind.* Washington, DC: Common Core. Available at http://www.giarts.org/article/why-were-behind-report-common-core.

[45] Arum, R. & Josipa Roksa (2011). *Academically Adrift.* Chicago: University of Chicago Press.

[46] Ravitch, D. and Antonia Cortese (2009). *Why We're Behind.* Washington, DC: Common Core. Available at http://www.giarts.org/article/why-were-behind-report-common-core.

[47] *Diploma to Nowhere* (2008). Washington, DC: Strong American Schools. Available at https://www.scribd.com/document/8534051/Diploma-To-Nowhere-Strong-American-Schools-2008.

[48] *Diploma to Nowhere* (2008). Washington, DC: Strong American Schools. Available at https://www.scribd.com/document/8534051/Diploma-To-Nowhere-Strong-American-Schools-2008.

[49] Jimenez, L. et al. (2016). *Remedial Education: The Cost of Catching Up.* Washington, DC: Center for American Progress. Available at http://genprogress.org/wpcontent/uploads/2016/09/30115238/CostOfCatchingUp2-report.pdf

[50] Bledsoe, Tyrone. Student African American Brotherhood. Saabnational.org.

[51] Shafer, L. (2017). *A Bridge Between School and Faith.* Harvard Graduate School of Education: Usable Knowledge. Available at https://www.gse.harvard.edu/news/uk/17/10/bridge-between-school-and-faith.

[52] Arum, R. & Josipa Roksa (2011). *Academically Adrift.* Chicago: University of Chicago Press.

[53] *Developmental Education Challenges and Strategies for Reform* (2017). Washington, DC: U.S. Department of Education. Available at https://www2.ed.gov/about/offices/list/opepd/education-strategies.pdf.

[54] *Developmental Education Challenges and Strategies for Reform* (2017). Washington, DC: U.S. Department of Education. Available at https://www2.ed.gov/about/offices/list/opepd/education-strategies.pdf.

## For Further Study

- Alexander, Michelle. The New Jim Crow: Mass Incarceration in the Age of Colorblindness.

- Barton, P. High School Reform and Work: Facing Labor Market Realities; 2006; ETS.

- Barton, Paul. One-Third of a Nation: Rising Dropout Rates and Declining Opportunities; 2005.

- Coley, Richard and Barton, P. Locked Up and Locked Out: An Educational Perspective on the U.S. Prison Population; 2006 ETS Princeton

- Hrabowski, Freeman, et al. "Beating the Odds: Raising Academically Successful African American Males (Oxford University Press, 1998)

- Lewis, Sharon, et al. "A Call for Change: the Social and Educational factors Contributing to the Outcomes of Black males in Urban Schools" Council of the Great City Schools, October 2010

- *Texas' School-to-Prison Pipeline: School Expulsion—The Path from Lockout to Dropout* (2010).

- Austin: Texas Appleseed.

# Organizations Doing Work to Keep Black Men in College

- The Schott Foundation
- My Brother's Keeper
- The Black Star Project

# About the Author

**Dr. Pamela Tolbert-Bynum Rivers** is founder and president of Steps Beyond Remediation, Inc., a 501(c)3 organization that supports adult students whose access to and success in college has been hindered by placement into developmental education, and Associate Professor of English at Naugatuck Valley Community College in Waterbury, CT. She received her doctorate from Teachers College, Columbia  University in Adult Learning and Leadership, with partial funding support from the Spencer Foundation Research Training Grant. She also possesses a Bachelor of Arts degree in English from Brown University, a Master of Arts degree in Biblical Studies from Regent University, and a Master of Education degree in English from Mississippi College. Her research interests are nontraditional adult students of color and low-income adult learners' college persistence rates, postsecondary education access, and post-secondary success factors for marginalized students.

She has contributed to the Bread Loaf Writers' Conference, is a recipient of the Puffin Foundation literary prize, created NEH curriculum for teaching Faulkner's *The Sound and the Fury,* served as a SAKS teacher fellow for the University of Mississippi's annual *Faulkner and Yoknapatawpha Conference,* and was selected to participate in the NEH Summer Institute *Four Centuries of Struggle: the Southern Civil Rights Movement.* Additionally, she is a 2013 National Institute for Staff and Organizational Development (NISOD) excellence award recipient and member of the 2017 *Harvard Women in Education Leadership* cohort.

CPSIA information can be obtained
at www.ICGtesting.com
Printed in the USA
BVHW08s0821170918
527707BV00023B/876/P

9 781933 435527